Democracy Days

DISPATCHES FROM THE OBAMA ERA

by John Wellington Ennis

ISBN 978-0-578-44396-6
Electronic ISBN 978-0-578-44602-8

For Dad, for showing me how to write,
and for Mom, for showing me what activism is.

Corruption's such an old song
That we can sing along in harmony

— Lin-Manuel Miranda, *Hamilton*

TABLE OF CONTENTS

Foreword

When I was a little boy, my parents would take me to downtown Chicago, and I would gaze awe-struck at the skyline, the river, the marble towers, the swarm of busy people. To see the city lit up at night, especially during the holidays, it seemed like a magical place that its residents must be so thankful for.

Growing up, though, it seemed like I saw nothing but bad news come out about this same beautiful city. Words like "alderman," "city council," and "the machine" became synonymous with words like "indictments," "pay offs," and "convicted."

I remember my mom teaching Sunday School, and asking all of us little kids to raise our hands if we liked one thing versus another. Noting that one child had raised their hand to vote both times, my mom joked, "Are you from Chicago?" Even as a little kid, I began to understand that Chicago's reputation for corruption was unrivaled.

I grew up resenting that. This beautiful city, that had been built by so many people from so many places over time, that had survived a fire, that had improv comedy, great parades, and the always-optimistic Cubs fanbase— this sprawling city with so many different types of people were not just being embarrassed by their leaders, they were being ripped off by them as well. I didn't yet understand what corruption was or why it happened, but it seemed to have something to do with accepting money and swinging elections, and doing so with the belief that you won't get caught. That was a thing that stood out to me as a little kid, the idea that this kind of crime wasn't robbing a bank or a thief holding people up, this was apparently a crime people were doing in their own offices against their own businesses. Why would you rob the people you work with, and then not even run away? Who *does* that? The outrage at leaders betraying who they represented stayed with me in everything I would end up pursuing. To me, corruption was the opposite of democracy, something we as humans will always be policing.

I confronted corruption how Chicago itself seemed to —through journalism and comedy. My senior year of high school, I was awarded my own column in the school paper, *The Evanstonian*, where I cherished my Royko-esque role chastising school administrators and President George H.W. Bush alike. That same year, I co-wrote our school's annual student comedy musical revue, YAMO, and strove to put in the same biting satire I had seen at sketch shows downtown that would stick it to Mayor Daley. Even though I seemed to be confronting corruption in 'The Chicago Way,' school officials were not amused.

At NYU, I wrote my first full-length script, *The Whole World is Watching!*, about the 1968 Democratic Convention in Chicago, when riots in the streets overshadowed a shoe-horned party process, and reporters were gleefully beaten by police. Out of college, I created a stunt comedy cable access show in Manhattan, *Toolz of the New School*, which began as a fun outlet for me and my friends, but grew into an ongoing critical platform of Mayor Giuliani's repressive "Quality of Life" campaign. As Giuliani's crackdowns worsened, a wider audience embraced out show for its dissent, and we were soon in newspapers, magazines, and on the Mayor's radar.

After moving to Los Angeles, I embarked on directing my first feature film, an improvised comedy with the Upright Citizen Brigade, *Wild Girls Gone*. While ostensibly a parody of the "Girls Gone Wild" franchise, the storyline centered on an opportunistic candidate espousing conservative values to cynically get into office. In our film, the fictitious town of White Sands, Florida, is a spring break capital, known for its world-famous ass contests. The town sheriff (Matt Walsh) is running for mayor, and to win the support of elderly voters, he bans spring break and outlaws the ass contests. His alcoholic housewife (Amy Poehler), who used to be the town's ass contest queen, has mixed feelings about her husband's betrayal of what they used to enjoy together, and goes about trying to subvert her husband's campaign by drunkenly starting ass contests around town. Even in a bawdy parody of spring break movies, I was able to work in an anti-corruption theme.

After learning how much work went into making a movie, I realized that if I was going to go through all that work to make a film, it should be about the most important thing I could possibly think of. So I set out to Ohio to explore what happened in the 2004 election, where thousands of voters were disenfranchised in a state that decided the election for George W. Bush. Through interviewing journalists, professors, lawyers, elected officials, local activists, and average Ohioans, I uncovered numerous schemes to suppress voters and defraud vote counts. I became so consumed with voting issues in this decisive state that I co-founded Video the Vote: a volunteer corps of videographers on election day to document polling problems or voter intimidation and report it using a new website called YouTube.com. We created a recruitment video for Video the Vote as a call to arms about two weeks before the 2006 elections.

Miraculously, our recruitment video took off, becoming national news, and I was suddenly seeing the video I edited on CNN with Wolf Blitzer, and doing double-takes while checking into some rural Ohio motel at the front page of *USA Today*, which reported on our efforts. We had tapped into a nerve, a deep concern for our democracy, and as we watched our local effort become a national team of thousands of volunteers, it felt deeply gratifying to see that there were so many out there who felt so strongly about defending the vote.

The resulting documentary, *FREE FOR ALL! One Dude's Quest to Save Democracy* was released in 2008, in an election year with plenty of voter suppression at play. My producer Holly Mosher insisted on putting the film online for free, at a time when streaming video was not easy. Our film received good coverage considering election fraud was a topic many were in denial about at the time. Roger Ebert wrote that the film was "engrossing, even enraging...Ennis has a lot to say." For all of its explosive allegations, nothing in the film was disproved; in fact, subsequent depositions confirmed some of the most alarming revelations.

My journeys through Ohio had produced an abundance of footage, and Holly had the foresight to see that we had a companion documentary to complete: the other major disenfranchisement in our elections, besides voter suppression, was money in politics. So we made another documentary about the challenges of running for office and how money played too big a role in elections, entitled *PAY 2 PLAY: Democracy's High Stakes*.

No sooner had we started a documentary on campaign finance reform, there was the biggest campaign finance upheaval in a generation: 2010's *Citizens United vs. F.E.C.*, wherein the Supreme Court decided that corporations had the same rights as people to spend money in elections. The issue of campaign finance reform came to the forefront over the next few years, while we worked on our film and tried to keep up with current events, like Occupy Wall Street or the uncovering of ALEC.

Released in the fall of 2014, *PAY 2 PLAY* had extended theatrical runs in New York, D.C., and Los Angeles, was hosted at the U.S. Capitol by Rep. Ted Lieu, and received hundreds of grassroots screenings in almost all 50 states. It is still presented in college classes and by democracy advocacy groups. I couldn't be more grateful.

Going in to 2016, it felt like we had the wind to our backs. Democratic candidates ran on overturning *Citizens United*, the main message from our film. Meaningful reform felt within reach for myself and the movement we had cobbled together with dozens of other democracy reform groups.

And then somewhere along the way in 2016—perhaps when the first violence occurred at a Trump campaign rally —there began a sinking feeling, a pit in my stomach, which is still there.

Much more will emerge about the truth of the 2016 elections, but as I write this, the DHS has confirmed that Russia hacked U.S. voting systems in numerous states.

Secretary of State Rex Tillerson says Russia is just going to keep trying to meddle in our elections and there's nothing we can do about it. The NRA has apparently laundered tens of millions dollars from Russia into the Trump campaign. Even George W. Bush—elected president only through widespread voter suppression in Florida in 2000 and Ohio in 2004—announced that it's clear Russia interfered with our elections.

Through most of 2017, I wanted to lie in bed. Sure, I marched, I put up street art, I use my social media to lend my voice to #TheResistance. But I kept thinking, what's next? Maybe this crisis will have stress-tested our democratic institutions, and they can someday be reformed; perhaps opportunists have already noted our institutions are really more like social norms.

Here's hoping we can someday pick up where we left off. My intention with this book was to preserve the writings and attitudes of an era when democracy itself was not being burned down, American sovereignty was not in question, and we asked how we could improve our electoral process instead of how to save it from Russian hackers and a complicit GOP. The Obama years certainly seem quite hagiographic for American democracy now.

Upon reviewing these essays about the Obama years, however, I came to remember an important truth: democracy kind of sucked, then, too. While we will always have eight years of a beautiful, scandal-free First Family to look back on, the reality was, our country was as fractious as ever. Republicans competed for the most openly disrespectful behavior toward the first African-American president. That Donald Trump's insulting demand that President Obama produce his birth certificate was even reported on by the U.S. media portended how much racist indulgence journalists would gleefully confront the president with. An entire movement popped up at once, calling themselves the Tea Party, predicated on a conservative course of government and reducing the deficit, which had not been a priority until there was a black president (nor has it been a priority since). This well-funded and coordinated right-wing backlash to Obama won Congress in 2010 and has held on since, sabotaging every effort at governance, from Speaker of the House John Boehner's forced government shutdowns to Senate Majority Leader Mitch McConnell denying Obama from appointing a Supreme Court justice. In this time, the Supreme Court struck down key parts of the Voting Rights Act and demolished campaign finance law.

So while President's Obama entire tenure may be recalled with less drama than a single week under Trump, it belies how much battling was really going on. In fact, the Obama majority was cut down even before it voted, when the Supreme Court supported Indiana's strict photo ID requirements in a 2008 decision, *Crawford vs. Marion County Election Board*, that would not go into effect until after the 2008 election. That law became the model for other states' laws aimed at making access to the ballot box more difficult, laws which cropped up like crabgrass.

America's arduous progress from a separatist slave state to its first black president was fraught with bad blood and spiteful decisions, much like we face today. I can wonder what it would be like to go back in time and convince the founding fathers to enshrine women and black people as equals, but the reality is, society wasn't ready. Each social movement needs its time to change society.

American democracy was revolutionary at the time, even though it only included white male property owners. American democracy is a work in progress. While Trump's boorish racism is in many ways the logical backlash to a well-educated, self-made African-American in the White House, foreign interference to affect the outcome of our elections is a whole new level of assault on American democracy.

Now more than ever, we need to keep the dream of democracy alive. The Obama years may not have been a perfect democracy, but it was a high water mark for inclusiveness in American history. In normal times, calling out corruption is not enough—we need to proselytize democracy as a value, as a way of life. It's not enough to observe democracy at that time of year when elections come around, like another holiday season we yawn through. We need to instill in ourselves and others that democracy is sacrosanct. We need to preach in support of inclusiveness while condemning the corrupt. We need to raise the expectations of what it means to be a good citizen, we have to glorify the good politicians, no matter how banal they are.

As idealized as the Obama years may seem, it wasn't that our democracy was healthy because the popular vote winner was in power. In fact, the backlash was swift and vengeful, but the glow of victory on Obama's election night kept us convinced that America was ours from now on. But it is on certain days that democracy gets a win—automatic voter registration going into effect in California, Pennsylvania's gerrymandered maps being struck down in court, a first-time transgender candidate replacing the

Assembly member that wrote North Carolina's anti-trans bathroom bill.

Democracy is something you have to fight for every day.

Preface

On January 18, 2018, I received an email from *The Huffington Post* announcing that the news site was discontinuing publishing posts from contributors. Launched in 2005 as a site that shared blogs by celebrities and pundits in the model of a salon hosted by Arianna Huffington, the site quickly grew to a news aggregator for the Left, ultimately to be bought by AOL and eventually turned into a less-colorful news portal with its own reporting. When I first started contributing essays and articles to Huffington Post in 2008, there was an air of prestige to being included. By 2017, after countless headlines about "nip slips," the prestige had long disappeared, and questions of paying writers for their work dogged the early adapter to the blogosphere. I myself had already decided to not contribute anymore, as contributor posts were no longer featured like they once were. But the end of the Contributor Era of HuffPost prompted me to reflect on the hundreds of articles I had submitted to what I considered to be the high school newspaper for grownups.

In that time I saw my articles quoted and linked in major newspapers in the U.S. and Europe. Once HuffPost started showing social media stats, you could see how many Facebook shares, likes, Tweets, or comments the article amassed, and it was possible to watch an article get hundreds of shares instantly. I used HuffPost as a platform to share videos of our movie-in-progress while working on our documentary *PAY 2 PLAY*, as well as writing commentary on how pay to play politics were unfolding around us. I was selected in a journalism competition to cover the 2012 Democratic National Convention for HuffPost and UStream, when streaming video was just barely viable.

This book is a collection of essays and interviews during the Obama era that appeared in HuffPost which are still relevant. There is still long-term reform of our voting systems and campaign finance laws to be achieved. In these essays there is unknowing prescience about the rise of the right wing as a backlash to Obama's election. The flash point that was Occupy Wall Street had to be experienced to be understood, but its captivating launch is relayed in these pages. There are writings that became curiously controversial and widely shared, like about the old TV show 'Dukes of Hazzard,' or even Ayn Rand, something you'd think was already well-worn. When hidden camera videos by some kid named James O'Keefe III emerged making wild accusations about ACORN, an established umbrella organization serving disadvantaged communities nationwide, I was one of the few to speak out immediately in the organization's defense and express skepticism about the videos. By the time the videos were found to be deceptively edited and illegally recorded, ACORN had been cut off from federal funding and disbanded. My articles were enough to catch the attention of O'Keefe, who claimed in his own book that I called him "the whitest guy ever." That I was quoting O'Keefe calling *himself* "the whitest guy ever" on FOX News shows how inherently disingenuous he is—and that he was apparently reading my stuff, too.

Which is the lesson I learned: you never knew who was reading. After I wrote a piece lambasting *The New York Times* for its bankrupting business decisions, Alec Baldwin wrote a passionate defense of the Grey Lady that read like a point-by-point response. I once hated myself for writing such a dumbed-down emphasis in a piece when I wrote, "This is serious stuff here," only to see it quoted in the *Washington Post* by Howard Kurtz, who thought it must be serious stuff. My diplomatic nudging of the intractable chair of the Ohio Democratic Party grew into a weeks-long controversy playing out in a small Ohio newspaper, fueling his resignation. There was the time I interviewed a conservative filmmaker about his Sarah Palin documentary, only for the exchange to boil over into battling columns on HuffPost, culminating in his think-piece, "John Ennis Thinks I'm a Dumbass: A Point by Point Response." Good times!

Here's hoping you enjoy them as well.

Dumb Politicians

CHAPTER 1

Bravo, Blago! A Primer in Pay to Play

01/10/2009

Bravo, Blagojevich! Amidst the awe-inspiring legacy of corruption you will leave behind (which takes a lot coming out of my hometown Chicago), you had the integrity and foresight to neatly distance "That One" from your middle-school mentality shakedowns.

President-Elect "Motherfucker," as you so fondly referred to him on federal wires, stands clearly out of the loop of your own pompous power grab. Your "fuck him" disdain for this historical politician who ascended from your home state not only keeps Obama the good guy, but your drooling over the Senate seat he left behind makes you look far less the leader of the Land of Lincoln, and more like a spoiled rich kid who inherited a prestigious family heirloom and ran to put it on Craigslist.

I am sorry you felt "stuck" as Governor of my home state, a job you rolled into fairly easily considering the outgoing Republican Gov. Ryan was going to jail for 6 years for corruption charges, and your Republican challenger to succeed him happened to also have the last name Ryan. (You just might be able to have too many Irish in politics after all.) Throw in your Polish-sounding last name to an electorate in Chicago where there are more Polish people than in Warsaw, and you, sir, just drew the lucky bingo card into Springfield.

So it might have been annoying to you that your name was despised by most Illinois Democrats so quickly, as you freely helped yourself to what was rightly yours as far as power, respect, deference, ass-kissing, money, favors, the like. So what if it was reported your own father-in-law wouldn't allow you in his home after you used him in your climb to the top?

Meanwhile, that pesky do-gooder Senator South Side, everybody loved him, they were already speculating about him "someday" as a presidential candidate. Everybody knows Governors have better odds at the White House, and you'd have to wait and plot your chance to 2016 for that gimme.

Beyond Blago's blindingly brilliant gift of that precious "plausible deniability" that Republican White Houses have shred countless careers for (paging Patrick Fitzgerald, care to comment?), he has further provided a simpleton's primer in The Way of Pay to Play.

One party rule (any party) breeds corruption like a big pile of fresh manure draws flies. Power unhampered, egos unchecked, oversight uncool — nobody wants to make waves and invite retribution from the only authority there is. And the non-empowered political and business leaders, as well as their electorate, they have to accept it and work with the system.

Two party politics proliferates Pay to Play. Without public financing of elections, only two (2) political parties get to make the rules for potential backers. And this happens in any state, at any level. While party-specific patterns emerge over corruption between Democrats and

Republicans — Democrats tend to go down over shameless shakedowns and sorry sex scandals, while Republicans go down over big-time cash crimes and gay sex scandals — these are two flavors of the same canned goods.

And when one party just temporarily looks slightly better than the other, it empowers that popular choice to make all the rules. Until hubris hits them hard, and then suddenly the eager business interests dart in the other direction like a school of fish. Over the years, in places like Illinois, Ohio, Washington D.C., it becomes a nauseous cycle of back and forth.

As an Obama staffer just wrote here on HuffPo, this new President is for everyone, not just you Progressives. We'll see if politics as usual breeds business as usual, or if our new leader can lead us all above petulant indulgence.

But we don't have to wait for that. We must get involved in our own local races, we have to take control of how our elections are funded, and we have to not let oafs like Rod Blagojevich believe they are the rule makers, when they are actually inheritors of the rules.

CHAPTER 2

Ken Blackwell for RNC Chair

01/16/2009

J. Kenneth Blackwell, the former Secretary of State of Ohio whose administration of the 2004 election made Katherine Harris look like Mary Tyler Moore, is aggressively pushing to become the next chair of the Republican National Committee when its 168 members convene in 2009 to figure out how to pull their party out of the deep, dank hole they have dug themselves into. And I for one support his selection wholeheartedly.

I have spent a tremendous amount of time studying Ken Blackwell. I made a feature length documentary which examines his corrupt stewardship of Ohio elections. Just a few of Ken's greatest hits:

- Purging a quarter of Cleveland's register voters, one of the most Democratic counties in the country.
- Rewarding no-bid contracts to Diebold for its voting machines, while owning stock in the company, your basic illegal conflict of interest.
- Going to court numerous times to make voting even more difficult.
- And when questioned about such anti-democratic maneuvers, the bellicose Blackwell emerges,

disrespecting the late, beloved U.S. Rep Stephanie Tubbs Jones.

But I'm not here to focus on Ken Blackwell's tireless war against democracy.

You see, in covering Ken Blackwell during his hapless bid for Ohio governor in 2006, I eventually realized that he requires another documentary to do justice to what a poor politician he is the rest of the time when he is not trying to subvert the electorate.

Here are some qualities the new RNC Chair should have, and how Ken Blackwell measures up to them.

The RNC Chair should be able to navigate past the party's previous losses and expand the brand appeal.

Since the election, many Republicans have stressed that the divisive platform of extreme conservatism not only drives away the expanding electorate, it limits the party's ability to talk about far more relevant issues. (Like the economy, stupid.)

Cut to Blackwell, stressing himself as a "full-portfolio conservative." His very word choice belies how he has amassed conservative credits like a starving actor on IMDB. His titles from the Family Research Council, the NRA, and more help to bury his opportunistic ascension through Cincinnati politics, starting as an African-American activist in college, on to the city council as a Democrat, to Independent, to fiscal conservative, to far right today.

His greatest conservative achievement is championing the amendment that banned same sex marriage in Ohio, even though two other laws previously existed against gay marriage. Blackwell has closely tied himself to the evangelical right wing base, and ratcheted up the heretic talk like he's the Spanish Inquisition.

The RNC Chair should have the respect of his party's leaders.

On page 347 of his book, *State of Denial*, Bob Woodward describes W.'s apparent fondness for Blackwell during election night, 2004, as he sat in the White House waiting for the election forecasts to swing his way:

At 2:43 a.m., someone noted that Bush was ahead in the popular vote nationwide, prompting the President to sneer, "If the popular vote made it, I wouldn't be here."

The campaign was left to anxiously wait for a statement from Kenneth Blackwell, a former black power student leader who had morphed into Ohio's gadfly Republican secretary of state.

"I'm the President of the United States," Bush fumed, "waiting on a secretary of state who is a nut."

And that was when Blackwell was delivering Ohio at all costs. Does Ken still think he's in the club?

The RNC Chair should know how to get votes.

Ken Blackwell lost his bid for governor by 24 points. His unpopularity dragged down the rest of the Republican ticket in 2006, sealing a takeover by the Democrats and ending the GOP's one party rule that had lasted 16 years. There arguably isn't a Democrat who could affect such a swing.

The RNC Chair should know how to wage an effective campaign.

Blackwell's strategy was simple: All negative, all the time. In the Republican primary for governor, Blackwell savaged his fellow cabinet member Jim Petro with ads that linked him with the Tom Noe pay-to-play scandal Coingate that had ruined the Ohio GOP. Lost in these ads were that Blackwell is also in the Ohio GOP, having also received money from the same Tom Noe, now serving 18 years in prison.

Bob Bennett, the Ohio GOP Chairman not normally known for prescience, had this to say about Blackwell: "A man who models himself after Ronald Reagan should have a little more respect for winning on ideas and vision. He knows the accusations in these ads are politically motivated, and this kind of guttural politics doesn't win votes. If we can't win with substantive ideas for leading Ohio, we don't belong in the race."

In the general gubernatorial race against the Democrat, U.S. Rep. Ted Strickland, Blackwell lagged in the polls the entire race. His strategy for a turnaround? In the final debate, Blackwell dramatically—however illogically—sought to tie his opponent to NAMBLA. The lowest of the low in scare tactics, it appalled Ohioans, and only cemented Blackwell's defeat.

The RNC Chair should know how to speak.

I am no Peggy Noonan (cough!) but I suspect that in debating an Obama administration, there will be a priority on eloquence.

Blackwell's call to arms in 2006 for civic involvement: "Whether or not we will choose to be thermometers that just take the temperature of our culture, or whether or not we will be thermostats to turn up the heat and define and shape and influence the morays of our culture."

Besides being uninspiring rhetoric (not to mention an incomplete sentence), this oft-repeated meme really just reminded Ohioans how expensive home heating had become. One camera crew I worked with in Ohio had just put in a wood-burning stove to fight their heating bills.

The RNC Chair should have a clue about using New Media to further the party.

Ken Blackwell is proud that he has a Facebook page, and that it even got coverage. What a techie! You'd think with such cutting edge technology such as "spell check," (like on my pirated Microsoft Word 97) he'd be able to spell his own name correctly as he lamely tries to tie Obama to Blago, which even most of the anonymous hotheads at Free Republic could do with more conviction.

Look at this cutting edge video from 2006 to see how he pre-dates Obama's Internet youth army. Just make a mock up of the MTV logo circa 1981, and those whippersnappers will be dying to go door to door for you! [Note: the video was made private after this posting]

In conclusion, I think most readers will join me in supporting Ken Blackwell to lead the Republican Party to a dismal future. Indeed, his penchant for election fraud may be their only chance left.

CHAPTER 3

Recalling Randy Hopper

08/08/2011

No. It couldn't be. Hopper?

The generic congressman headshot grinned back indifferently, like they all do. Only looking at the Facebook profile pic of Wisconsin State Senator Randy Hopper, a Republican facing a looming recall election and public divorce, did I recognize that impenetrable grin. Had it been 25 years?

As the Wisconsin GOP unleashed attacks on public employees and unions this year, I was sickened by the shameless pandering of Governor Scott Walker, who had given away hundreds of millions of dollars in tax breaks to corporations before using that same deficit amount as an emergency pretense to slash state workers' benefits. I was even more disgusted by the lengths to which the Wisconsin GOP went to pass a vote against political foes, breaching their own state assembly procedures to enact a drastically unjust law that takes away citizens' rights — from a party purporting to be against big government intruding on your life and limiting what you can earn.

The Wisconsin GOP kept up its bare-knuckled tactics of passing the law with tens of thousands protesting outside the statehouse, with the state's Democrats out of state in absentia. This law was just struck down by a judge in Wisconsin precisely for the improper procedures that went into passage of the bill. Then the Wisconsin Supreme Court re-enacted it.

No sooner had the Wisconsin GOP got their business-friendly agenda passed than the recall petition drives started against the GOP leaders who had supported this corporate coup. Further signs of the backlash came in the hotly disputed State Supreme Court election, which has been marred by outlandish claims of election officials, broken chain of custody of votes, and statistically impossible anomalies — all of which have helped the Republican candidate, who will be acting as the state's oversight.

With their time in office looking limited, the Wisconsin GOP passed strict voter ID laws, a requirement that is well known to disenfranchise poor and minority voters, as well as college students. These are demographics that tend to vote against Republicans. Voter ID laws are always justified with claims of voter fraud, despite the lack of existence of voter fraud year after year. It's a bully tactic to make it harder on people to vote. To low-income people who rely on public transportation, requiring the purchase of a state driver's license amounts to a poll tax.

And after requiring an ID only obtainable at DMVs, Republicans tried to close down DMVs in poor areas.

And then the misleading voter mailings from the Koch Brothers' Americans For Prosperity told voters to vote after the day of the recall elections.

Wisconsin had already become a banana republic before the suspicious fire that burned down the headquarters of We Are Wisconsin, the opposition organization of that sprung up in response to the insatiable power plays of an unpopular minority.

But none of this had a face on it until I happen to just recently see the full name of one of the state senators facing a recall election on August 9th. This particular recall election was one of several that Republicans pushed back from July 15th, costing the state tens of thousands of dollars more.

Reading the name "WI State Sen. Hopper (R)" means nothing to me. But once I saw a tweet mentioning the name Randy Hopper, it felt like something out of a movie. Specifically, Animal House, at the closing epitaphs, where John Belushi's character is driving off in a convertible having just sabotaged a parade with a hapless co-ed in the back: "Sen. Bluto and his wife live in Maryland, Virginia."

I had heard of a Republican state senator in Wisconsin who was facing a recall election at the same time as a divorce. His wife left him after he began sleeping with a 25-year-old staffer for whom he later found a job. Learning that this was indeed Randy Hopper, it seemed all the more like a mediocre comedy with Adam Sandler playing a caricature of a clueless politician.

Randy Hopper was a counselor at my summer camp. Red Arrow Camp is an all-boys sleep-away cabin style sports camp on Trout Lake outside Minocqua, Wisconsin. I went there three summers, for seven weeks spanning from June to August. There were just over 100 boys, aged from about seven to 14, living maybe nine to 12 in a cabin sleeping in bunk beds. Each cabin had two counselors who were usually college aged. Randy was not my cabin counselor, but was an instructor for numerous activities, coached for different sport teams, and often addressed the campers collectively. He'd gone there as a camper himself, and took pride in RAC. Everybody knew everybody, and Randy was often the center of attention, even among the other staff.

And I mean everybody knew everybody. In what now no doubt sounds like a homoerotic fantasy, all boys bathed in the nude collectively in the lake, every night, sometimes in the morning too. It seems like something from "Mad Med" that back then, we regularly shampooed and soaped in the lake where it spilled in to a river. But eco-hindsight aside, the most daunting part beside the cold water was the showcase of puberty, and who was manly enough to be showing hair growth.

In an all-male environment, many civilized norms can start to slip away. It became commonplace in camp for counselors to address campers while resting their hands down the front of their pants. Randy in particular was a natural at returning his hands to their natural resting position over his scrotum. (This was commonly referred to as "making goop.") And yet, nothing ever really seemed perverted, just devolved.

This was an environment where early strains of macho take shape. What made you matter to the other boys was being the best at sports, having done more with girls than others, and not attracting ridicule. This I did not particularly succeed at, and tended to focus on lesser-respected activities like photography and theater.

Randy was a really good athlete. He could run a 50-yard dash in under six seconds. He played lacrosse at Marquette, and was a big deal there. He taught me how to play lacrosse, calling it the fastest sport on two legs.

Randy coached me at other things. He was probably the best water skier, helped no doubt because his family had a ski boat of their own. Randy was from a wealthy family in that area of Wisconsin, not a suburban explorer from Illinois like most of the kids. He was gregarious, often funny, a big presence among little boys. Though sometimes intimidating with his authority, he could still connect to the little kids that looked up to him. I was quiet around him, but admired his coolness.

Randy was my coach for the annual flag football tournament in camp, called The Salad Bowl. The process of preparing for the Bowl was half running plays and covering basic football skills. The other half seemed to be a focus on psyching out your opponent through glares and taunts, along with motivational speeches to make this flag football game very important to us, culminating in the whole team listening to a tape of inspirational music before the big game, which was songs from Rocky and dramatic classical music.

When our team won and ran off to the lake cheering, I remember being really happy — for Randy. I was glad I hadn't let him down, I was proud that he was proud, and I hoped he might think I was cooler.

Randy was a good storyteller. He disclosed to us on occasion the camp's problematic history with a murderous disfigured local known simply as "Hook Man." Hook Man had acquired this name because of the large sharp hook where one of his hands should be. Hook Man had used this appendage to kill wild deer and campers, ran surprisingly fast and quietly, and had even stalked a former counselor who had to leave the camp, as Randy explained to us in hushed tones around a camp fire late one night. Many of the cool boys would continue to insist that Hook Man was real for the remainder of our time at camp.

Once a week the camp would get together in the main hall at night and sing songs. We read the words off a typed slide projected from a massive old projector. Randy would lead us in songs like "Lean On Me" or "He Ain't Heavy, He's My Brother." The values of this traditional boys camp were deeply instilled in us, and its website today still reflects the principles I learned there: "Red Arrow aims to inspire every camper to live unselfishly, thoughtfully, confidently." Randy was perhaps the biggest advocate for Red Arrow and encouraged appreciation for the tall pines, waking up with the bugle in the morning, and displays of sportsmanship.

We would occasionally play a neighboring camp at softball, and Randy was our coach. The bus ride over he would be drilling into us how much better we were than the other team because of our discipline and tradition. We wore matching shorts and t-shirts for our games. The other camp wore over-sized tie-dyed T-shirts. And when they managed to beat us despite their unkempt appearance, Randy would tell us on the bus back to camp that how they behaved upon winning was unbecoming, and that we represented ourselves well.

Randy Hopper gave me my first Grateful Dead T-shirt. It was a Jerry Garcia for President shirt, reading "Garcia in '88." I didn't know who Jerry Garcia or the Grateful Dead were at 12, but the shirt was cool because it was his, and I was psyched to be able to have stuff he wanted to trade for it. It was the first of many Dead shirts I would wear until Jerry died in 1995.

Randy was my coach for the camp's annual Olympics events, where the camp was divided into teams named after countries, like Italy, France, or America. We were Germany. While our team was lined up on a long bench outside our mess hall, talking about who wanted to compete in different events, I noticed Randy look at me and mutter something to the other counselor. Something was jotted down. I didn't know what that meant.

I later found out. I had been put in an event without knowing what it was. It felt helpless, and the event scared me to death. The Individual Medley. I was never a good swimmer, I was even taking swimming lessons with the little kids because I was still fearful in water. The Individual Medley, which I had never heard of, consists of swimming one length freestyle, one length scissor-kick, one length backstroke, one length breaststroke. I didn't even know how to do all of these strokes. Not only was I going to lose and be the only team out of four to not get a medal for this category, I was going to be so far behind the other guys swimming, when they finished I would still be flailing with a style I never tried, with two more lengths to go. I would be humiliated, mocked, teased, outcast.

I pleaded with Randy afterward and he refused to change the assignments. I told him how I had a better chance at any other thing, I was bad at swimming, I didn't know the different strokes. I was on the verge of tears. He walked away. I cried about it in dread. I prayed that if there was a God, that if he could do anything that could get me out of doing this, I would always believe in him and be grateful. (Either somebody heard me, or jet streams were on my side: a massive storm blew through, with high winds, barraging rain, and violent waves. For the first time in the camp's history, the Olympics were canceled because of bad weather.)

It was then that I saw how someone charismatic that everyone listens to can be dangerous and scary to me. Particularly when they can do whatever they want.

I can see the early signs of a future politician in my summers with Randy Hopper — popular, always talking to groups, a cunning storyteller. But I am so deeply disappointed that this is the guy I knew who taught me such values as sportsmanship, teamwork, empowerment through challenges, a sense of community. He helped me to love Wisconsin. How could he be a part of all this? What a betrayal of all we prized. This depresses me all the more as my work in recent years has been dedicated to election integrity and campaign finance reform.

When I think of the people Randy Hopper represents now, I wonder if they care about his politics, his party's tactics, his personal life, his upbringing, or don't care about him at all. Maybe they have seen enough undemocratic grabs at staying in power. Maybe they really want to pay more to private services for things the government has been built to offer free to taxpayers. Maybe his constituents will vote for him to stay because they fear no one is fighting hard enough to give tax breaks to billionaires, even if it means stripping worker rights, slashing public services and cutting jobs.

I don't think these Wisconsinites care so much if their state senator was a showboat asshole summer camp counselor. There is no salacious gotcha-type smearing in the vivid memories I have from a camp that was as much recreation as rite of passage. This is perhaps a portrait of where future power poachers breed an ideology that they can disavow with growing leisure.

Because the reality is, the assault on voting rights in Wisconsin has made the voter suppression of the 2004 presidential election in Ohio look like miniature golf. Where many focus on get-out-the-vote efforts, I believe the votes will already be at hand to recall these embarrassments to elected office.

This clash is a turning point for America between bullies who keep getting their way and the will of an already suffering people. Because if they could, they would do like Randy Hopper's Germany and put you wherever they want, regardless of what you say or do.

CHAPTER 4

Democracy in Ohio is Hard Enough Already

10/01/2014

Democracy in America is such that, after its citizens have participated in national elections, and all of their votes have been counted, with each state's combined number of U.S. House Representatives and Senators determining an allotment of Electoral College votes, added together with due diligence reveal — reliably — that it all comes down to whichever way Ohio goes, every time. The rest of the country is at a disadvantage during national elections; Ohio has become our de facto kingmaker.

In 2006 I set out to understand the state and its quirks for a documentary, which turned into two. Three statewide elections later, I have seen how not only is Ohio a prognosticator for the rest of the country, but in order for our democracy to work, we need a fair political process in this state more than anywhere else. Achieving this is like the entire country working to thread a needle.

I was looking at the costs of running for office, but observed how there can be considerably bigger barriers to running for office — your own party members. A former statewide candidate described how he learned that his campaign materials, paid for by good Democratic donors, were destroyed routinely at the behest of the Democratic

Party Chair, who was pushing his own guy in the primary. That this was the candidate of color whose campaign was sabotaged by his own party makes it all the more disquieting.

Such bare-knuckled tactics should be revolting to those who believe in a democratic process, who cherish the American dream of open and fair elections. Thwarting candidates in the primary undermines building a party, by only offering the Good Old Boy Network approved choice, when primary participation is already so low for the most pivotal voting. By limiting or derailing their own candidates for office, the Ohio Democratic Party prevents participation and discourages new interest. Instead of clearing the field for minimal opposition, a party leader might be better off building a stable of popular contenders, like a professional wrestling franchise.

And today, in 2014, we have the same Chair of the Ohio Democratic Party openly disparaging his own party's nominee for governor just a month before the election. Not mocking your own candidate at the top of the ticket is a tip they teach in law school. Just kidding, nobody teaches that, because it is so fucking obvious.

In a new poll, the current Democratic candidate for Ohio Governor, Ed FitzGerald, netted 35 percent of the expected vote. He was not the first choice for Democrats, as the previous governor Ted Strickland was expected to run again against John Kasich. But when Ted Strickland abruptly decided he wasn't going to run in 2014, suddenly there was an opening at the top of the ticket. Chris Redfern, the Ohio Democratic Party Chair, told *The New York Times* that no other major Democrats stepped up to run for governor.

Yet when another potential contender sent his chief of staff around Ohio to solicit support from Democratic leaders for a possible gubernatorial bid, the party leadership swatted away the overtures of one who would dare run against Ted Strickland. Such defiance leads to threats against others to disavow the persona non grata, and future leaders are outcast. Participation in the democratic process should not be a scorched-earth process.

Looking at the current Democratic gubernatorial candidate distracted by the curious revelation that he hasn't had a drivers license in a decade, wouldn't Ohioans prefer to be able to vote for the head of Elizabeth Warren's Consumer Protection Bureau, who also happens to be a Jeopardy champion?

Instead, Republican Governor John Kasich, who was humbled just a few years ago in a two-thirds statewide vote smacking down his anti-union legislation — brought to you by ALEC — Kasich is now setting his sights on the White House.

Moreover, the effects on the the rest of the down-ticket Ohio Democratic candidates is disastrous. Important candidates like State Senator Nina Turner, campaigning hard for Secretary of State, will lose the turnout they need to win their races. In the battleground state of Ohio, where the current secretary of state's efforts to reduce early voting was just supported by the Supreme Court, this is the kind of race that determines future presidential elections. Did Hillary Clinton plan on winning Ohio?

Over the years of making these documentaries, a number of would-be candidates have told me that they cannot run while Chris Redfern is chairman, because he has ostracized them and put others on notice that they are disloyal to the party if they dare side against him. It's like potential candidates are getting mugged before stepping out the door to run for office, already a thankless undertaking. These kinds of rivalries, how-dare-you-question-me-I-banish-thee, these are the kinds of feuds propagated by a Palin.

Perhaps it is incumbent on me to raise these issues because as an Angeleno, I don't fear retribution from a vindictive party boss. And yet, if I am aware of these long-simmering problems from three timezones over, this discontent is probably no secret.

All of this makes more sense when you consider that Redfern did not enter politics with lofty ideals of empowering the common man or the gratification of public service, but rather, as he bluntly put it to me in an interview, he joined the College Democrats to impress girls. Whose party is this in Ohio?

If Redfern's behavior only mattered for colorful documentary material, that would be one thing. But the reality is, this is a vindictive individual suppressing candidates and their potential supporters. If we are to weave a new era reflecting the interests of people instead of corporations, we can't even thread the needle if citizens are bullied away from participating in our democratic process in the most pivotal state of the union.

How can you have democracy in Ohio when you can't even have democracy in the Ohio Democratic Party?

CHAPTER 5

In Midterms Aftermath, a Bright Spot in Ohio

11/07/2014

Elections have consequences. And in the most decisive state in the nation, the 2014 midterms have already produced measurable improvement.

In the wake of Republicans' easy victories Tuesday, Chris Redfern announced he would be stepping down as the chair of the Ohio Democratic Party. The writing had been on the wall for Redfern in recent weeks, whose snide comments the Ohio press had become inured to. But when Redfern mocked his own party's candidate for governor to *The New York Times*, what had been an open secret of an abusive relationship between a man and his party finally had to be confronted.

The role of the state leader for the Democratic Party has repercussions far beyond one election, in one state. In this election alone, handing the Republicans an easy win elevates shoddy public servants to the next tier of their aspirations — for Gov. John Kasich, he can set his sights on the White House, simply because he can win Ohio, which is all you need to win anymore. Secretary of State Jon Husted looks to follow in his predecessor Ken Blackwell's footsteps, applying his game of voter suppression in his own race for governor.

Redfern's commitment to bullying away potential Democratic candidates as disloyal was well-known. The nominating convention in which he was first coronated as ODP chair was rife with dissent and threats, with those who dared seek the leadership position chair ostracized as persona non grata. Petty and vindictive, it didn't take much to get on his bad side, and it never seemed to be about ideology or policy, more about his people above others. The Democratic Primary became an empty exercise in posturing, as eventually no one seemed to be challenging any of the party picks for some reason.

So when *The New York Times* asked Redfern why the chair of the Democratic Party was resorting to abandoning his thinly-vetted nominee for governor, he demurred that no one else stepped up to run after Ted Strickland opted to not run again. Of course, to those who recall Redfern's isolation of Richard Cordray for gauging support for his own potential gubernatorial bid, this claim of Redfern's was simply more wash for hogs. The noncompetitive race in Ohio allowed the Republican Governors Association to pour more money into other state races, which they won, as did pretty much every candidate with the most money.

Ohio is still a 50/50 state. John Kasich had his ass handed to him at the polls just a few years ago when two thirds of the state soundly rejected the anti-public worker laws that were from the ALEC bill mill. In this bellwether state that serves as an eerie prognosticator for sentiments around the country, Chris Redfern lost his own seat in the Ohio House, losing to a first-time candidate who is a suspect in a burglary. The typically defiant Redfern, known for a Twitter presence so combative he used a skull and crossbones as his avatar, deleted his social media accounts immediately after the election, announcing he would step down in mid-December. Some in his party have pondered: why wait that long?

An Ohio newspaper asked Redfern about allegations made in my documentary that Redfern destroyed campaign materials of a Democratic candidate during a primary. Redfern denied any such thing, suggesting I lied and that I never sought his response. Unfortunately, Redfern's refusal to give me an interview in 2010 after I learned about these staggeringly anti-democratic tactics doesn't help him now that the movie is out. And since the film's release, yet another candidate in the film told me that Redfern did the same to thing to their campaign.

Whatever new leadership rises from the smoldering rubble of Redfern's ODP, it will be clear that the party has to be inclusive, it must encourage many different voices to attract more supporters, and, like the college football that Ohio is freaking obsessed with, they have to work like a team.

PART TWO

Money in Politics

CHAPTER 6

Our Pay to Play System, Embodied by Beanie Babies

09/23/2014

There was a political scandal I heard about that changed the way I looked at corruption and helped me understand the larger mechanisms at work in government and society. It rocked the swing state of Ohio right after a disputed election, toppled the state's one-party rule and ended the Taft legacy that included a President, a U.S. Senator, a Supreme Court Justice. And it started with Beanie Babies.

In Toledo, Ohio, Tom Noe was a small-time rare coin dealer who sought to raise his business prospects by getting involved in politics. He would later testify under oath that giving money to politicians "kept my business alive." Noe elevated his status as a political player by bundling contributors together in North East Ohio in order to get more attention from statewide candidates. Warm and gregarious, Noe would volunteer as campaign manager for State Supreme Court candidates and take the entire governor's office out to dinner at Morton's Steak House down the street (it was dubbed "The Noe Supper Club"). Noe's goodwill earned him impressive appointments, being the only individual to serve on both the Turnpike Commission and the Board of Regents, an especially impressive role in directing higher education statewide, considering that Tom Noe had dropped out of college after his first year.

Of course it did not stop there. The Ohio Bureau of Workers Compensation, an in-state insurance fund contributed to by employers, oversees a sizable investment portfolio, in the billions, and as such diversifies its holdings with fiscal strategy. At some point it was deemed a good idea to create an investment fund of $25 million, and then an additional $25 million a few years later, at the discretion of Tom Noe's business empire, which at that point consisted of a hobby shop in a Toledo strip mall.

During his trial, the government would testify that Noe used this BWC fund as his own personal ATM. The list of things Tom Noe blew this money on would make a sheik blush. It wasn't just the waterfront homes, party boat, Corvette, new pool, it was also political collectibles, like a Christmas card signed by JFK that was highly valued, or a letter signed by Richard Nixon that was not as highly valued.

And guess where even more of that money went, based on this personality profile presented thus far? That's correct. Back into more campaigns. Tom Noe was the top Republican fundraiser in Ohio, throwing himself a 50th birthday roast that featured the entire Republican ticket as his guests of honor. In the end, because it is so hard to parse where the money went once it went into Noe's pocket, Governor Taft was hit with ethics charges over much more minor infractions, albeit provable ones — not declaring golf games as gifts that Tom Noe paid for.

And when it came to become a Pioneer in the George W. Bush campaign by raising over $100,000, Tom Noe couldn't let the opportunity pass. He roped in as many friends as he could to make it happen so that W. would come to see HIM, in Toledo, in front of everybody. Not everyone could fought that up though. So Tom said, "Okay, put in what you can, and I will give you the rest." This generosity, commonly known as money laundering, involved up to 28 individuals, several of them elected office holders who knew exactly what they were doing.

When investigators into missing funds from the BWC found over $13 million unaccounted for in Noe's records, it was all the more remarkable as to what did comprise Noe's $50 million portfolio of Ohio funds: Rare coins. Beanie Babies. Le Bron James jerseys. George W. Bush shot glasses. You know, collectibles. When some of these coins came up missing, that didn't help, as did records presented by his partner in court proving that some of the coins never existed.

And yet, the coins that did exist in this fund? They appreciated. This was in part because Tom Noe had gotten a special deal to remove taxes from coin shows in Ohio. This brought the coin industry to Tom Noe's door, and cost the state $50 million is lost revenue, the same amount he was given by the Ohio BWC.

When it all came crashing down, the Republican office holders that benefited so richly couldn't run far enough from him. The lingering investigation details of what would be known as Coingate made Tom Noe a household name statewide and led to a Democratic takeover of the State House in 2006.

Tom Noe went to State Prison for his fraud and embezzlement, and is now serving in Federal Prison for his Bush campaign donations through others' names. (For whatever reason, Dinesh D'Souza will not get prison time for doing the exact same thing.)

But in the end, this taught me how Pay to Play costs us all. While Mr. College Dropout was joking about hurrying up for the snacks at education forums, Ohio education floundered, causing "brain drain," when the best and brightest flee the state for better opportunity. This is the state that decides our elections.

I set out to tell the story of Coingate and thought it said everything about politics and how it all goes back to the cost of running for office, making candidates reliant on big donors who expect a high return on investment. But as the ripples of the scandal ushered in a new era, I became transfixed on what other obstacles keep outsiders from having a voice, which became a much bigger story. But in the end, divorced and serving back-to-back sentences, only the Beanie Babies are still around for Tom Noe. Because when you play in Pay-to-Play, we all lose.

CHAPTER 7

Who is Citizens United?

01/20/2015

As we mark the 5th anniversary of the disastrous Supreme Court decision *Citizens United vs. FEC*, it is worth heeding: Who is Citizens United, and how did they manage to subvert generations of campaign finance laws? The name now synonymous with untold billions influencing our elections had its origins as a much more meager offspring in the same spirit of under-the-table politicking.

In 1971, Lewis Powell, a corporate lawyer, wrote a pivotal essay outlining manifold ways that large business interests could engineer a corporate takeover of the democratic process in America in order to maintain their dominance. The Powell Memo, as it came to be known, called for vast lobbying by businesses as well as industry-wide trade groups, creating think tanks to author business-friendly policy, acquiring media outlets and newspapers that will promote that business idea, as well as a long-term gaming of the legal system to fight regulation with the corporate war chest. Another recommendation of Powell's was to foster and support independent outspoken groups to lend the appearance of popular opinion supporting the business-friendly agenda as it makes its way through the co-opted outlets, because even he knew these ideas were not popular. Powell's new treatise earned him the admiration of industrialists, and he was swiftly appointed to the Supreme Court by President Nixon.

Jump to 1988, the presidential race between Vice President George Bush and Massachusetts Governor Michael Dukakis. With Dukakis ahead by double-digits coming out of the Democratic National Convention, it would take something considerable to derail his momentum against the candidate with the Iran Contra scandal hanging over him. The Republican National Committee released a campaign commercial of its own, which marked one of the first times an outside group ran its own TV ad, particularly to do the dirty work for a campaign.

This ad, "Willie Horton," became legendary both for its incendiary racial pandering as well its divisive success. Using the mug shot of a black man with a beard, a grave announcer told the story of how this man stabbed a boy and a girl after being released on furlough under Gov. Dukakis, whereas George Bush supported the death penalty. A false choice to begin with, this notoriously manipulative ad neglected to mention that this furlough program was founded by Ronald Reagan when he was governor. The racist fear mongering was deliberate, from the fact that Lee Atwater changed his name from William to "Willie" to sound more uneducated, to GOP political consultant Roger Ailes' infamous quote, "The only question is whether we depict Willie Horton with a knife in his hand or without it." (Roger Ailes now runs FOX News, by the way, I'm sure Powell would be proud.) The provocations of prejudice proved effective, elevating Bush to President, and also cementing a future of outside ads—with outside money —to operate as an extension of the campaign, often being the knee-capper out of nowhere.

Floyd Brown, who co-created the Willie Horton ad, went on to found Citizens United that same year, 1988, to continue the effort of conservative trolling in the modern political landscape. The group was quiet for the first few years, until they ran ads attacking Senate Democrats who were considering against confirming Clarence Thomas for the Supreme Court, as he was mired in controversy surrounding sexual harassment. David Bossie joined Citizens United as Floyd Brown's protege, leaving Capitol Hill where he worked as an aide for Newt Gingrich until some of his efforts to smear the Clintons had gone too far, which is saying something.

From there, Citizens United churned out home movies of talking heads espousing conservative sentiments covered with stock footage. Some videos were Reagan hagiographies, others demonizing the ACLU and the U.N., even Bossie's mentor Newt Gingrich hosted a few of their films. That is essentially the level of where this non-profit 501(c)(4) Citizens United was — if Newt Gingrich has some publisher that will print his 16 books or how ever many he has banged out, think of this as the home video version of the small-market conservative press.

Notoriety did not arrive until Citizens United ran ads for *Hillary: The Movie* in New Hampshire within 30 days of the 2008 primary, violating campaign laws as a non-profit running political spots. While the ads were ostensibly for the movie, the commercial itself consisted of lacerating accusations against Hillary Clinton, clearly intended as an attack ad.

Four years prior, David Bossie had claimed that movie ads for *Fahrenheit 9/11* were technically ads for John Kerry's campaign, since they showed President George W. Bush, John Kerry's opponent. When the Federal Elections Commission denied that Michael Moore's movie ads were the same as outside ads in elections, that set the stage for Bossie to attempt the same claim.

After Citizens United were fined by the F.E.C. for the New Hampshire ads, they took the government agency to court, claiming that their commercials for a video-on-demand should not have been subject to the restrictions outlined in the McCain-Feingold Act of 2002. But once it reached the U.S. Supreme Court, this case took a dramatic twist.

Citizens United, the group, is just one viper in the pit lurking to strike against a fair democratic process—they happened to strike at the right time, after years of advancing ideologue judges deferential to corporate needs over the public interest. While the Powell Memo proved effective, it is prefaced on the belief that People Power ultimately guides our country. On the fifth anniversary of *Citizens United*, the energy and support for major reform has become a widespread effort, attracting citizens across the political spectrum. Let this day mark as an anniversary of uniting us behind the necessary, inevitable reform ahead.

CHAPTER 8

What is Pay to Play?

09/10/2014

What is Pay to Play? Commonly held, pay to play is a form of getting a special deal because you paid someone off. Usually this is an indirect transaction, because of clear legal guidelines, and so creative ways are devised around long-standing common-sense laws prohibiting politicians from taking bribes. For instance, when Virginia Gov. Bob McDonnell was asked to testify in his corruption trial as to who gave him a lavish Rolex watch, the governor artfully pointed out the gift tag stated "from Santa." Plausible deniability, indeed.

But while the McDonnell tragicomedy may be the stuff of Lifetime movies, the reality is, there is not much difference from a first family taking goods to endorse a company than when a candidate for office takes thousands of dollars in campaign contributions from those who expect a personal return. And since the Supreme Court's Citizens United decision removed limits to outside spending in elections, the TV ads that dominate political campaigns are basically unregulated as far as spending or disclosing who is paying for them. As we have already seen with Super PAC sugar daddies like Sheldon Adelson, one billionaire with a bug up his ass can get presidential aspirants pirouetting.

And so it is with anticipation that we witness an historical event this week in the Senate, where a debate was held over introducing an amendment to the Constitution that would undo some of the shock waves from Citizens United. Scheduled to be brought to cloture by Sen. Harry

Reid Thursday, the Democracy For All Amendment is a tag-team of amendments introduced by Rep. Jim McGovern in the House and by Sen. Tom Udall in the Senate. Down the road, this would then have to clear the House of Representatives, where it is sure to pass like a kidney stone.

Yet while this issue of money overwhelming the political process may need debate on Capitol Hill, the rest of the country has been in agreement for some time that reform is needed and that their elected officials do not prioritize their constituents' interests.

From political newcomers in the swing state of Ohio, to activists on the front lines protesting ALEC, to L.A. street artists risking arrest and injury to get their message up, I've found many people speaking to the same inequality in different ways, and using their voices boldly to make a profound impact. It may be hard to envision how our actions and words can be so interconnected, like ripples in the ocean.

While we may have our debate in Congress this week in an unprecedented pushback to *Citizens United*, we have larger reforms to achieve in order to ensure the dream of democracy this country is always striving for. Here is a modest proposal for how to put an end to our pay to play system through six substantive reforms.

FIX SIX

1. **Public Financing for Campaigns**. Candidates should be listening to the voters, not the donors. Public campaign models exist in this country already and around the world.

2. **Disclosure**. Part of free speech is accountability for your speech, and those trying to conceal their political

spending usually don't want people to know because it won't be popular.

3. **Free Airtime for Candidates**. Already in practice around the world, the public airwaves belong to the people, and should be available in more than 30 second segments that distort the debate.

4. **Required Voting (Like Jury Duty)**. Numerous countries like Australia and Brazil already require citizens to vote in elections. And if you think about it, concerns about "voter fraud" would be appeased because now every person is responsible for their own vote.

5. **End Gerrymandering**. Redistricting has let politicians choose their voters instead of voters choosing their politicians.

6. **A Constitutional Amendment** affirming that Money is not Speech and that Corporations are not People. Because the Supreme Court's definition of corruption has been whittled down to a *Choose Your Own Adventure* Book.

These reforms are a start, and not easily achieved, but I believe as our society evolves, these steps toward democratic inclusion will become a popular demand that drives our national experiment into a thriving new era.

CHAPTER 9

Keeping the Heat on Clarence Thomas

07/10/2011

While the Supreme Court started its summer recess last week, watchdog group Common Cause is keeping the heat on Justice Clarence Thomas. In two separate actions on Thursday, July 7, Common Cause has drawn further scrutiny to an already embattled judge. Sitting in a lifetime appointment on the highest court of the land, the controversial behavior of Clarence Thomas is drawing increased calls for the Supreme Court to be held to the same code of conduct as all federal judges.

In the wake of a *New York Times* article chronicling Justice Thomas's relationship with billionaire Harlan Crow, Common Cause filed a Freedom Of Information Act request to the U.S. Marshals Service for details of jet and yacht travel that Harlan Crow has provided Justice Thomas, as well as other gifts.

Americans are concerned, and rightfully so, over mounting evidence that our highest court is operating outside the ethical standards that apply to other federal judges," said Common Cause President Bob Edgar. "We are seeking records from the Marshals Service, which typically provides security for justices traveling outside Washington, to clarify whether Justice Thomas has violated federal ethics laws. We hope to engage the legal community in a larger effort to bring ethical accountability to the full court.

In another attention-getting move, Common Cause took the need for the judicial code of conduct to the professionals that abide by it — the American Bar Association. In a letter to ABA President Stephen Zack, Common Cause president Bob Edgar urged the largest association of lawyers to take a position on Justice Thomas's potential conflicts of interest, and to help persuade the highest court to embrace the code of conduct adhered to by all other federal justices.

In his letter to Zack, Edgar wrote:

"Our system of justice depends on public confidence that those administering the laws are also following them — in letter and spirit. While the Supreme Court is at the pinnacle of the justice system, and only it can enforce the rules on its members, it is vital that respected, legal organizations such as the ABA make their views publicly known on such critical matters as these."

Common Cause recently submitted a letter to Congress signed by 135 law professors urging the adoption of a comprehensive code of judicial ethics applicable to the Supreme Court. Common Cause even wrote Chief Justice John Roberts, known to fancy himself an umpire calling fair and foul, to seek his opinion about judicial ethics.

Common Cause has been pressing the issue of judicial impunity since ThinkProgress reported a leaked invitation to an annual conservative retreat by Charles Koch advertising that Supreme Court Justices Clarence Thomas and Antonin Scalia had been past presenters.

Further investigation into Clarence Thomas's financial records revealed that he had neglected to report his wife's additional income from conservative groups that stood to benefit from cases before the court. In a report by Politico, Harlan Crow was identified as the donor of $500,000 to Ginni Thomas's political group, Liberty Central. Crow also reportedly spent $174,000 to add a wing named for Justice Thomas to a library in Savannah and put down $1.5 million to purchase an abandoned cannery where Thomas' mother once worked in Pin Point, GA, to build a museum about the cannery.

Edgar notes that Justice Thomas has acknowledged failing to properly disclose his wife's sources of income over a 21-year span, a violation of the Ethics in Government Act. "Now, there's evidence that the justice also may have failed to report, or misreported, travel paid for by a wealthy friend," Edgar said. "This is a serious matter. The Ethics in Government Act provides both civil and criminal penalties for willfully falsifying or failing to report required information on annual financial disclosures. The reports are the only way lawyers, litigants and the public can check to be sure that the justices and lower court judges are not taking part in cases in which they may have a conflict of interest."

In a statement, Common Cause chronicled a timeline of Thomas's travel surrounding his interaction with Crow, pointing out legal requirements to disclose such gifts.

The *Times* also raised questions about whether Thomas has traveled on Crow's corporate jet and yacht without reporting it on financial disclosure forms. Federal flight records indicate that a Crow-owned jet flew in April 2008 from Dallas to Washington DC and after a brief stop went on to Savannah, where Crow's yacht was docked. During that same week, an item appeared in a South Carolina publication noting Thomas' arrival aboard Crow's yacht in Charleston, SC, a few hours north of Savannah. Thomas reported no gifts or travel reimbursements in that time period.

The *Times* noted two other instances in which Justice Thomas's travels corresponded to flights of a Crow-owned plane. Justice Thomas was in Savannah in early 2010 for the dedication of a building in his honor. On the day of that event, Crow's plane flew from Washington to Savannah and returned to Washington the next day. Justice Thomas reported in his financial disclosure that his travel had been paid for by the Savannah College of Art and Design, which owned the building.

In a 2009 financial disclosure, Justice Thomas reported that Southern Methodist University in Dallas had paid for him to travel to its campus for a speech on Sept. 30. Flight records show that Crow's plane flew from Washington to Dallas that day.

In reviewing flight records, Common Cause discovered four additional trips in which a Crow-owned plane traveled from Dallas to Washington and after a brief stop went on to Savannah. In three of those trips, the plane then reversed its route to return to Dallas, again stopping briefly at Dulles International Airport in the Washington suburbs. On one trip, the plane returned straight to Dallas.

Federal law requires that Supreme Court Justices, like all federal officials, disclose who pays for their travel; intentional misreporting is a violation of both the Ethics in Government Act (5 USC 104) and 28 USC 1001.

CHAPTER 10

Taking a Stand Against Money in Politics

04/02/2014

Democracy was blindsided four years ago in *Citizens United* when the Supreme Court gave an answer to a question it was never asked. What began as regional TV ads for an on-demand movie somehow let the Supreme Court undo a century of campaign law, insisting that no amount of money could corrupt a politician. The results have been disastrous—our electoral process has become an open market place for politicians to be bought by billionaires' Super PACs.

The Supreme Court issued a new ruling on election spending Wednesday that could sabotage our democratic process further: McCutcheon vs. Federal Elections Commission. That the Supreme Court even decided to hear the case over whether aggregate campaign contributions should be limited to "only" $123,600 indicates that the Roberts Court is poised to exacerbate the problem of money in politics.

We're not going to take this lying down. That's why thousands of us are organizing for a national same-day response to the McCutcheon ruling. The news of the ruling may be bad, but the news of the day can be a powerful statement that Americans are taking a stand against Big Money taking over our political process. Right now over 200 events are planned around the country for the same day response to McCutcheon. The response has been percolating, evidenced by the unprecedented recent video recording of an activist from 99 Rise proclaiming to the court that money is not speech and corporations are not people.

I've been documenting the toll that money in politics takes since 2006, and in that time, I've seen more and more citizens recognize how virtually all of our problems stem from this inequality, and step up to make this the fight that matters the most to them. And if you look around, you'll see that Americans are doing what they are best at, taking a stand in the name of justice.

From the momentous clean money campaign reform just debated in New York State, to California's disclosure law, to the 16 states that have passed resolutions calling for a Constitutional Amendment, citizens are finding ways to counter the negative impact of money on our self-governance. I have hope because more and more people are standing up.

History repeats itself (or, if you will, time is a flat circle). Over a century ago, President Theodore Roosevelt said, "All contributions by corporations to any political committee or for any political purpose should be forbidden by law." This led to the Tillman Act of 1906, specifically intended to free politicians from relying on the petulance of corporate benevolence, and likewise allowing businesses to no longer have to pay a form of extortion to greedy statesmen. This concept survived a hundred years with updated legislation, as recently as this century from the McCain-Feingold Act.

But it was at the behest of Chief Justice John Roberts —who during his confirmation hearings likened his role as Chief Justice with an umpire calling balls and strikes—that the home video company Citizens United expand their argument before the court from one about pay-per-view ads in New Hampshire to a much broader case about the regulation of all corporate money in elections. This overreach by one judge with a lifetime appointment was like a lance through generations of hard-fought reform by rivaling elected leaders that worked together for the mutual survival of their dreams for democracy. For an umpire, Roberts seems to fancy himself the Commissioner, free to rewrite the rules as he likes.

The *Citizens United* ruling unleashed corporate money, and now the McCutcheon case may allow an individual to give $3.5 million to candidates and campaign committees. Do you think your Congressman will listen to you, or the guy who gives millions?

We have fought this fight before and won. As recently as Watergate there was a generation of reformers who helped establish the campaign finance laws that ended the "suitcases of cash" from the Nixon era. And We, The People, can override the agenda of an aggressive jurist. That is accomplished with an amendment to the Constitution, the 28th, which states that money is not speech and corporations are not people. And that starts by taking to the streets when the McCutcheon verdict is read.

Take a stand, find a McCutcheon Decision Day protest near you, or start one of your own. Even if its just you standing on a corner with a sign on the day the media will be filled with news of the next *Citizens United*, you'll be one of thousands across the country, sending a powerful signal that people matter more than money in our democracy.

CHAPTER 11

Playing Monopoly With Our Lives

09/22/2014

In all likelihood, when you were little, you played America's best-selling board game, Monopoly. The colorful money, antique tokens, and cartoon old man let us pretend to be important, to feel successful, to realize the American Dream of prosperity. This childhood memory becomes something parents share with their children, growing into a cultural touchstone spanning generations.

Perhaps it is the warm memories of playing with siblings that obscures what the game's objectives are, how it is played, and the lessons it imparts. For one, there is the object of the game itself, plainly stated: The winner is the last player left in the game, having driven their opponents into bankruptcy.

Just recently, Bank of America agreed to the largest court settlement in history: $16 billion with the Department of Justice in a wide-ranging lawsuit over the bank's collateralized debt schemes. Do you think that the executives at Bank of America that engineered these schemes believed that robbing their customers was okay because it meant they were getting ahead by bankrupting others? You have to wonder what kind of monopoly mindset breeds such betrayal of the client.

And you also have to wonder why any of these bankers won't be held accountable, considering this was orchestrated by people who knew better. Yet, corporate personhood means that fingers can be pointed in countless directions, plausible deniability abounds, and the defense of "I was just following orders" seems to get everybody off the hook. Corporate personhood is the ultimate get-out-of-jail-free card.

Even the very rules of Monopoly violate anti-trust legislation that has been in place for generations. These are the kind of laws that helped America grow and thrive, like preventing corporations from discriminatory pricing in railroad shipping. This is the same Interstate Commerce Act cited in the Supreme Court's ruling over the implementation of the Affordable Care Act (aka Obamacare) as to whether or not the federal government can be involved in regulating state health insurance programs. Those who were mad that others' healthcare was not taken away are probably the same ones who prefer to own all the railroads and utilities in Monopoly, clucking at others' misfortunes.

The recent anniversary of Occupy Wall Street reminds us of the basic inequality that compelled so many to take to the streets spontaneously in protest. While "We are the 99%" became the rallying cry for demonstrators, the lop-sided distribution wherein 1 percent of the population owns over 40 percent of the wealth wasn't even the real outrage. More specifically, the target of ire were those among the top one percent that use their money to rig the system in their favor still more, generally through political spending. It's not so much about being against rich people as it is being against rich people buying government.

Yet we learned in Monopoly that not only is hoarding wealth the American Dream, but that the banker can take money as needed to keep the game going, much like the executives who gave themselves obscene bonuses from federal bailout money after crashing the American economy. What's more, in Monopoly, there are many unwritten rules known only by experts, like trading properties or bidding on open squares. For most Americans, not being clued in to insider rules is an unfair disadvantage, allowing trusting citizens to invest in worthless derivatives, presume a bank won't try to steal their house, or believe that their elected leaders actually care about their constituents instead of their contributors.

Because while corruption has long been born from candidates' need to fill their campaign coffers, the role money plays in politics today has reached crisis levels. The public's contempt for politicians has reached new heights, between their relentless fundraising and the negative ads they buy, with a bipartisan majority believing their representatives don't listen to them. The 2010 Supreme Court decision *Citizens United* allowed corporations to spend unlimited money in elections without having to disclose its origins, opening up a new era of Dark Money that fuels our elections with unknown motivations — because if those motivations were known, they probably would not be popular.

But there's one motivation for dark money that you could probably guess, and it is reason enough to worry: a return on investment. Just like when you build houses and hotels on your squares in Monopoly to extort jacked-up rents from other players landing on your properties, pouring money into politics through lobbying and campaign donations pays back manifold. From deregulation of industry standards (also known as "decriminalization"), to tax breaks, to government contracts, to federal giveaways, the return on investment from political spending averages a whopping 22,000 percent, according to a study published in the Journal of Law & Politics. Is it really a capitalist market when the marketplace is rigged by those who paid more to change the rules in their favor? Is it really a democracy when people's votes matter less in elections than corporate spending?

No matter how much the Supreme Court may dilute the definition of corruption to a meaningless term, by insisting that no amount of money can corrupt a politician, the larger injustice doesn't seem to matter to these justices: Beyond the right of an individual to spend as much as they want in elections, what about those who cannot afford to max out contributions? What the court has said in *Citizens United vs. FEC* and again this year in *McCutcheon vs. FEC* is that might makes right — that our rules should be curtailed to benefit the very richest, that the biggest spender deserves the biggest latitude, and that the only voices that matter are those that can afford to dominate the discussion.

So how do we escape this real-life Monopoly? Well, for starters, it might interest you to know that the game of Monopoly as we know it is itself a corporate lie, an appropriation from the public domain that inverted lessons meant to teach the dangers of real estate monopolies. Realizing that we have grown up with a lie for our favorite childhood board game is symbolic of the larger questions we must ask ourselves about how much we let corporate hegemony control our society.

The official story of Monopoly's invention reads like Horatio Alger, a success story of man trying to feed his family during the Great Depression. In 1932, as the story goes, Charles M. Darrow conceived of a finance board game with intricate rules and colorful squares that let the gamers play mogul. After Parker Brothers first turned down the game, they saw that it was catching on in department stores as Darrow made copies himself, so in 1934 they acquired the rights to the game. The game got bigger and bigger, making Darrow and his descendants fabulously wealthy.

Since Darrow lived in Philadelphia, it might have seemed curious that the squares in this game were named after Atlantic City streets. While Darrow would maintain in his correspondence with Parker Brothers that he conceived of the game all by himself, Parker Brothers had been hearing that there was already another game from their sellers, and it was just like the Monopoly that Darrow claimed to create.

Flashback 30 years. In 1904, a patent was registered for a board game called The Landlord's Game, to a woman named Elizabeth Magie. The game featured squares of property, with different prices, going around a board, with the object being the accumulation of property. Players could buy, trade, and auction off properties as they managed their burgeoning real estate empires. There was a Park corner, a jail that players could be sent to, and cards that kept the game moving.

But The Landlord's Game was designed to teach. Lizzie Magie had been a follower of the Quaker economist Henry George, who strove for equitable distribution of wealth in society. Among George's lessons that Lizzie Magie wanted to impart: the idea that increasing the value of property creates a bubble because it offers no new wealth or commerce. The notion of a real estate bubble imploding is not so far-fetched today.

The Landlord's Game was so popular, it continued to spread for decades even when the game went out of print. Friends taught each other the game, even making their own board games from wood or oilcloths. The game was particularly popular among Quakers, who modified the rules to make playing more conducive to the Quaker lifestyle. From homes to schools to a Quaker orphanage, the little changes made to the Landlord's Game (also known as "finance," or "monopoly" with a lower-case "m") became integral to the eventual popularity of the game.

So when Charles Darrow was introduced to the game and then passed it off as his own, it would take corporate intervention to monopolize this property. Imagine what would be involved if you tried to claim inventing "cards" or "chess."

This background and the man who uncovered it, Ralph Anspach, appear in my new documentary *PAY 2 PLAY*, which looks at our modern system of pay-to-play politics like a game of monopoly. I wanted to tell his story in my film because I found that the original folklore had been reinforced so much by the makers or Monopoly that when I told people their childhood game was a corporate lie, no matter how jaded people were at politics and corruption and greed, their reaction was almost always shock: "Not Monopoly!" That outrage is the spark to action.

Because we need to get past our jadedness and doubt that what we say or do has little or no impact. Our stories spread and grow because of the human connection between us. The hundreds of thousands of people who took to the streets of New York for the Climate March are using their voices to make the call to action louder than ever. They obviously weren't there because of the corporate media.

CHAPTER 12

Pulling the Wool Over Our Eyes

11/05/2014

No one likes having the wool pulled over their eyes. Now imagine wealthy CEOs hiring millions of knitters to blanket your entire city with a massive wool sweater, soaked in gasoline. That's what dark money is. It's rich interests that already have millions to burn, but would rather spend that money on polluting our election process and muffling the public's voice. And they are going through ever-greater hoops to hide the source of the money in this election cycle, precisely because people seeing the truth is bad for their cause.

What our founding fathers and mothers set forth in America was an experiment in democracy, one that seemed daring at first independent of a monarch, but soon needed to enfranchise the rest of its citizens. To those that came before us, who sought to build a better life for their children, the right to participate in our democratic process was paramount to what it meant to be free.

So to see how broadly cynical our election process has become, with stealth spending groups unleashing torrents of ads and mailers with deliberately false information, it makes a mockery of a sacred civic participation which our countrymen died for. It is sad that it should come to this, but the reality of today's governance is that spending money in politics offers a greater return on investment than any other form of enterprise — up to $22,000 percent according to the *Journal of Law & Politics*, and at the state level that ROI is doubled. You and I might think it unconscionable to turn a room full of people raising their hands to vote into a showroom of masked people shouting at you. But then, corporations have no conscience.

While the Roberts Court continues to look out for the rights of corporations to spend unlimited amounts in elections as if they were entitled citizens, one thing corporations don't have is a conscience — just a board of directors and shareholders with fiscal quarters and fluctuating stock prices and rival companies of their own. Somewhere along the way the consequences of group decisions perpetrated through bureaucracies have real impact, from plundering public resources to courting corruption. If a person had no conscience, no remorse, and was driven by nothing more than survival, their destructive tendencies would match the behavior of a sociopath. This is the part of personhood that the Roberts Court is committed to recognizing in corporate privilege — some of humanity's worst traits.

So the idea of a wealthy sociopath that cannot be sated using our local and national elections as a means to manipulate your basic municipal functions — that should scare the crap out of you. Wouldn't you like to know about that? Outside attack ads have come a long way since the infamous "Willie Horton" ad was run by the RNC in the 1988 presidential race, instead of by the George Bush campaign. The younger Bush in 2004 would squeak by in a narrow election with the help of outside ads so maligning and mendacious, they became a verb in our common parlance: Swift-Boating.

According to a study by the Center for Responsive Politics and *The Huffington Post*, dark money — expenditures by groups that refuse to disclose their donors — the biggest source of this dark money has been the Koch brothers, Charles and David. Their network of groups have spent a combined $52 million in House and Senate races in 2014. Considering their combined net worth tops $100 billion, that amount might seem like chump change to them. Karl Rove's Crossroads GPS just spent $26.2 million of dark money, with a 96 percent success rate, and him spreading falsehoods in an election is like a kid in a candy store.

What America needs, and deserves, are meaningful disclosure laws, because if money is being considered speech, speech comes with responsibility, and there are consequences for those who falsely yell "Fire!" in a crowded theater. We need people-powered candidates that can compete with massive out of state anonymous spending. We need local party members to cultivate engagement and future leaders in their community. We need to work with and compel the FEC to respond to the concerns of citizens, instead of being the whipping post for lawsuits aimed at rewriting laws without the legislative branch.

When our country was founded, there were founders who abhorred slavery, but had to accept it as part of the revolt against England. If you were an abolitionist at that time, you likely would not be alive to see slavery outlawed once and for all after the Civil War. But there's no doubt that those who spoke out against a commonly-accepted practice had an impact. Every voice matters, and it will take each voice to bring about the next era of reform.

CHAPTER 13

This is Exactly What Pay to Play Looks Like

12/13/2014

Our new film *PAY 2 PLAY* is centered on how our political process is bound invariably by big money interests who use campaign spending as bait for politicians to get massive payouts in return from the public piggy bank. As Noam Chomsky explains at the beginning, "Both parties are two factions of one party—the Business Party." I've learned that Chomsky's mere inclusion makes the film seem too "liberal" for some, coupled with the refrain: "Why can't you show both sides? If you showed both sides, then it might be more persuasive to (party label here)."

Choosing sides in an election is secondary to achieving a real democracy in the first place, so that everyone's voices are included. Today, half the country doesn't vote, and half of Congress are millionaires. The inclusive component of what makes America special has been under siege for decades, by people who already have lots of money, and seek to use our government to make themselves even richer. To show "both sides" in this context is to have a billionaire explain that even as the middle class suffers, he intends to use the Republican Congress which he spent a fortune to help elect cut the hell out of spending, balance the budget, reduce regulations, and support business. This actually does appear in our film, when Lee Fang interviewed David Koch celebrating the first day of the Republican Congress in 2011. Koch had just spent money helping elect 1,053 candidates out of 1,216 winning candidates in 2010.

The other gasp of concern comes from passionate activists on the left, who ask, "The two parties are the same? How can you say that? One party denies climate change, supports torture, the other supports women rights and equality..." and you know the rest. In *PAY 2 PLAY*, we see populist candidates undermined by their own party leaders. We see vanity candidates who are self-financed that don't really believe in anything except that they should be in office, and lying is a good way to get there. We see the effects of low voter turnout. There are so many other obstacles in the road to an open democracy.

The reason we use the number two in our title *PAY 2 PLAY* is not an homage to Prince lyrics, it is because we have a two-party system, and you have to pay either (or both) political parties if you want to participate. There might be two different buses that want to go in two different directions, but they both run on the same fuel: campaign cash. Endless amounts of it. And this week the U.S. Congress approved a spending package with so many kickbacks and give-aways, in the words of the Great Curtis Scagnetti, it's more rigged than an S&M pirate ship. This is what this "CRomnibus" is, an S&M pirate ship.

Calling it craven doesn't begin to do it justice. More like a re-imagined Disney show, "That's So Craven," this spending bill is a stunning piece of pay-2-play™ at the hands of both parties, despite Elizabeth Warren and Nancy

Pelosi making powerful stands against it. While we posit in our film that Insiders versus Outsiders are the "both sides" we should be addressing, who could better make that case now than the Insiders themselves, the incumbents? Somehow, in the hundreds of pages necessary to fund the government, someone tripped and fell and dropped this bit of legislation in: party contribution limits were suddenly raised ten-fold. How messed up do you have to make campaign finance laws that even Citizens United denounces it as a gratuitous incumbent incentive? Our elected representatives agreed with no debate that the government couldn't function without jacking up contribution limits for how much their parties can receive. That shit is deep.

Even deeper shit is the paragraphs that were written in this spending bill not by some elected leader or their staff, but by Citigroup, to rollback financial regulation without hearing or deliberation. That backdoor action is literally pay-2-play at its purest: those millions that Citigroup has put into lobbying and contributions could reap them billions. Jack Abramoff makes this clear in our doc: "The return on investment is astonishing." Putting money into politics is a bigger return on investment than Wall Street. That's why Wall Street is writing our legislation.

Combined with bonus features like attacking unions and overruling a local election, this trillion dollars spent by leaders from heavily-gerrymandered districts makes this Cromnibus a Pay-2-Play Parade.

Our film unfolds around a reimagined monopoly board, likening the richest-takes-all board game to the contest of winning elections The thesis of the film is stated ten minutes in: "If we could learn the rules of the game, maybe we could find a way outsiders could win." Taking back our democracy starts with taking back our elections. That's achieved through People Power. As John Nichols explains, "If you want to challenge the money power, you are going to have to build People Power. For every million dollars they spend, you're going to have to get a thousand people. It's not easy. But it is necessary." We can circumvent the impacts of big money in our election process, but it takes people getting involved at every level, like a chain of hands running through your community.

Politicians love to get in front of a parade that is already underway. Let's make that parade. Let's make the fight to #GetMoneyOut cool. I can't help but view this naked grab at money as a conscious last mouth-stuffing, because they know their time is coming to an end.

CHAPTER 14

How Doug Hughes Took Free Speech to New Heights

05/19/2015

Doug Hughes does not have a Super PAC.

A Super PAC, created in the wake of the 2010 Supreme Court decision *Citizens United vs. FEC*, is a campaign expenditure entity that has no limits to how much money it can spend in an election or how much one donor can contribute to it, but it cannot give money to a candidate, and it cannot coordinate with their campaign. Granted, that term "coordinate" is pretty loosey-goosey these days, as Jeb Bush's Super PAC has largely supplanted his campaign for president, which he hasn't even bothered to declare yet, since that would require following "rules" by the Federal Elections Commission, which even the FEC Chair says can't be enforced anyway.

Doug Hughes has not been a major campaign contributor.

Indeed, according to FEC records, Doug Hughes has basically failed to exercise his free speech in the form of giving money to politicians. In fact, all the other Doug Hughes-es put together pooled a paltry $20,000 in political contributions, far short of the amount of speech that only one (1) Shaun McCutcheon has to spend, who had so much to say that the Supreme Court saw fit to rewrite the laws again in 2014 so that the Alabama coal executive could spend millions in contributions to candidates.

A U.S. Postal Service worker, Doug Hughes has been a public servant, and in his time has seen campaign mailers proliferate, while voter registration cards dwindle. He's seen his invaluable agency attacked by lobbyists looking to sell off the Post Office to private interests. As a government employee, Doug Hughes might well have felt entitled to share his thoughts with other government employees, specifically elected officials in Washington, D.C. After all, the Constitution makes it very clear that Congress works for the American people.

Ah, but here's the rub. Doug Hughes wanted to share his views with Congress about issues affecting the country as a whole. But, if you've been reading closely, you already know that Doug Hughes does not have a Super PAC, nor is Doug Hughes a major donor, nor is any other Doug Hughes that he could even hope to be confused with. On a government employee salary, Doug Hughes did not have a media conglomerate or fossil fuel factory of his own, for whatever reasons.

Yet, Doug Hughes wanted to address this very dilemma: That because elected officials focus all of their efforts on raising vast amounts of money for re-election, and because corporations have come to write their own legislation, our country needs new campaign laws and a constitutional amendment to reclaim our democratic process from the highest bidder. Members of Congress could either accept this and reform the system, or deny it and fight reform.

As it turns out, a number of people have been up in arms about pretty much the same things. From op-eds, to books, to protests, to teach-ins, to occupations, to ballot initiatives, to movies, to a movement for a constitutional amendment, Americans across the political spectrum are demanding reform of our campaign finance system. But when over 50 percent of Congress are millionaires, they can be oblivious, like refusing to raise the long-outdated minimum wage while wanting to raise their own salary.

Doug Hughes did not have a Super PAC. He did not have the clout of a major donor. But he did have a gyrocopter.

As a candidate for office, you have to raise hundreds of thousands of dollars just to get your message out. It's already hard on candidates, but if you are a citizen trying to get a message out? What, are you going to rent your own billboards, or get your own airtime?

Doug Hughes knew something about getting airtime. Not the media buys that have become so pivotal early on in campaigns — actual airtime, like a hang glider with a propeller, at a tenth of the cost of a helicopter.

After a couple years of stewing on the idea and amassing gumption, Doug Hughes followed through on his own personal dare: becoming the mailman for Congress, delivering his own letters to each individual member of Congress urging immediate action on our pay-to-play system of politics. Doug Hughes chose Air Mail, bringing his letters from Florida, and delivering them personally to Capitol Hill, by way of a one-man air mission, which was covered nationally as breaking news.

Because let's face it: would a non-wealthy person get attention from the media or Congressional staffers without making an arrival that would undoubtedly get their attention?

As Doug Hughes faces charges that could put him in jail for four years, the most serious of which is operating an aircraft without a pilot's license, his case must be tried for the larger issue of free speech that is at stake. The flight of Doug Hughes was a form of nonviolent direct action aimed at raising awareness about the urgency of campaign finance reform. Because none of our most pressing needs will be faced until we get the corrupting influence out of the way. So vital was getting this message out, Doug Hughes risked his life to share it with his country.

And as long as the Supreme Court interprets "free speech" to include spending untold fortunes in elections, it seems fair to also define free speech as a peaceful protest on public grounds, or even public airspace. Because just as Supreme Court justices have long interpreted the First Amendment to say that in elections, you can't really say much without spending money, the flip side is presented here — since you can't really say much without money, you have to speak out in different ways, such as a very public demonstration.

The question should not be, how could Doug Hughes pull such an ambitious stunt just to make a statement? We need to ask ourselves the much bigger question: what other recourse did he have?

CHAPTER 15

Movement to Reform Campaign Finance Keeps Growing

06 / 03 / 2015

Reform rarely arrives as a silver bullet, clearing danger in a single shot. The way reform takes hold is more gradual and disparate, like ivy or tree branches growing, until one day you notice all the leaves you are surrounded by.

With the Run Warren Run campaign now retired, progressives will look for a new hope to upend the system. Even as Hillary tacts continually leftward, calling for a constitutional amendment in response to *Citizens United*, Bernie Sanders has stepped up to run for president on the very inequality that most Americans are most concerned about, according to a new CBS/*New York Times* poll. "Almost three-quarters of respondents say that large corporations have too much influence in the country."

In another new poll from CBS/NYT, most Americans recognize our campaign finance system for what it is, a morass of wealth and influence drowning out citizens voices in elections:

"By a significant margin, they reject the argument that underpins close to four decades of Supreme Court jurisprudence on campaign finance: that political money is a form of speech protected by the First Amendment. Even self-identified Republicans are evenly split on the question."

Some seek to minimize these findings, because of a caveat included in the NYT article: "Virtually no one in the poll ranked campaign financing as the most important issue facing the country." I could speculate that if you asked Americans what was the most important issue facing the country in 1800, virtually no one would identify ending slavery. That doesn't mean it is widely-held as profoundly wrong, it's just seemingly impossible to change.

Many Americans think things are impossible to change because not enough people feel the same way they do. But what if they found out most people shared their feeling— that the U.S. campaign process needs fundamental overhaul just to begin to try to be fair? When our Congress can't reliably agree to keep the government open?

Here is a harsh truth about this movement to reform our campaign finance system and why you won't hear much about it on TV, like when a promising amendment is introduced into the 114th Congress: because networks make so much money from campaign ad buys, media conglomerates aren't really looking to upset the business model anytime soon. Local TV stations in Ohio during campaign season can just run a full hour of ads, and forgo programming altogether, because they make so much more money from inflated ad rates—ads on publicly-owned airwaves to begin with.

Even when a grandiose movie moment happens in real life, such as Doug Hughes spectacular arrival at the U.S. Capitol on April 15 via gyrocopter, the media will all but censor his clearly stated intent of delivering letters to Congress demanding they act on campaign finance reform.

Capitalizing on the loaded suggestion of "mailman" in the headlines, news outlets overlooked his explanations about needing a constitutional amendment in response to Citizens United. Yet there was virtually no coverage of how Doug Hughes had the book thrown at him, facing up to 9 years, and is now being let go by the U.S. Postal Service for his demonstration.

But like Doug Hughes has found, he is not alone, many others are working away without being the subjects of reality TV shows. From Washington to Florida to California and everywhere in between, Americans are working on the state, county, city, and local levels on reform. If you put your ear to the ground, you can actually listen to the dissent growing.

PART THREE

Voter Suppression

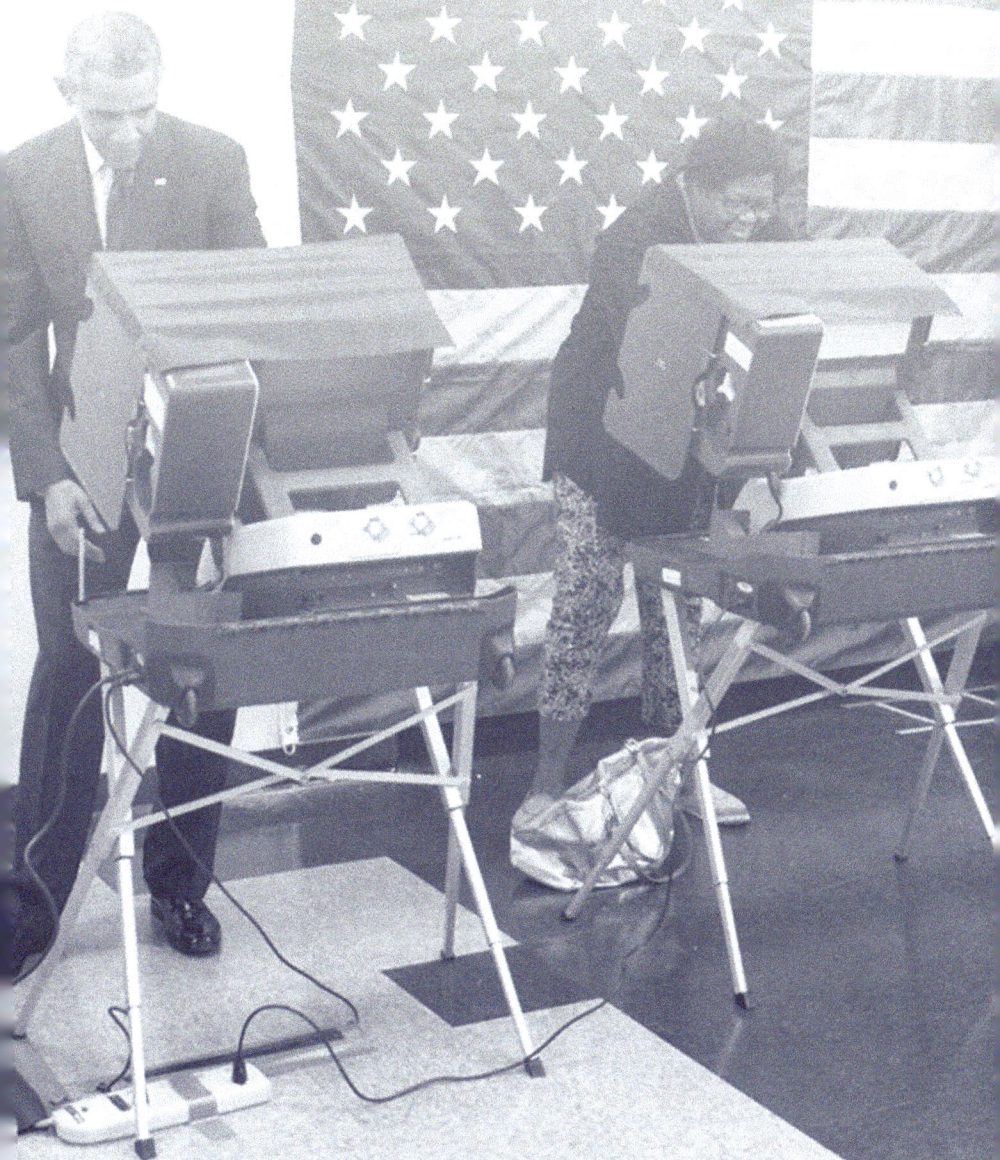

Photo by Pete Souza

CHAPTER 16

The Technical Term: Human Error

October 2008

A video went wildly viral, produced by my group, Video the Vote. It showed a county clerk in West Virginia demonstrating the reliability of his county's ES&S machines when they are properly calibrated, versus out of calibration in response to complaints from early voters that they saw their vote flip from Democrat to Republican.

This helpful official gladly took our camera through the process of what voting machine calibration looks like. (Think of a Palm Pilot or an iPhone, you tap the screen in certain places so it gets its bearings.) After showing how alarmingly off the votes will register without proper calibration, the county clerk rebooted the ES&S voting machine, re-calibrated it, and showed the difference in the reliability of the touch screen.

In voting for Ralph Nader, then selecting the straight Republican ticket afterward, he noticed Ralph Nader was still selected as his choice for president. He immediately said the machine was still out of calibration, moments after assuring us that it was calibrated properly. Note, the Nader vote should have stayed as it did. This county clerk was mistaken. Out of our recent series of reports on voter rights (Video the Vote) in different states, the traffic for this video suddenly skyrocketed.

The Attorney General's office and the Secretary of State of West Virginia called us up, threatening legal action for misrepresenting their machines. There were edits in that video, and it didn't show the full process. The machine was right; the county clerk had been wrong.

We got calls from the Associated Press, *Computerworld*, *Wired*, all wanting to know the context of the vote flipping. Was Video the Vote sensationalizing this clip? While people had believed that these machines might be deliberately switching their votes, this just turned out to be a video of simple human error.

Exactly: Human error. What these tech experts and election officials are too close to see is that human fallibility is just one of the reasons that electronic voting machines are a disastrous idea. Besides the widely documented security flaws, besides the tendency to break down and cause lines, besides the outrages costs of our tax dollars, there is the also the fact that the average poll worker age is 72, and may not be up to speed on DOS. Which is the even bigger problem with these electronic voting machines. An overwhelmed poll worker, this county clerk, even the Secretary of State of West Virginia can't even look inside these voting machines. They're protected by trade secrets, the software is confidential, and the private company of ES&S are the only ones who knows for sure what goes into their machines. If any other industry suggested that to banks, casinos, stock traders, they would be laughed out of their sales meeting. I for one do not blame the county clerk forced to defend and recalibrate this computer system. If he had paper ballots, which anyone can see and don't disappear when you unplug them, he wouldn't be explaining the circumstances where people see their votes register differently than they intended.

What I fear people debating this video are missing is in many of the thousand or so comments on this video. Reactions like: "Why should this even have to be calibrated? Why can't I vote on something more reliable after all the daily technology we use like ATMs?"

Look, I'm not a tech guru. I am just some dude. I was fed up with not trusting our political process, so I went out with a camera through Ohio to find out if our elections are subverted. Over the course of my journey, I joined with other activists and filmmakers to launch Video the Vote in 2006 to capture election problems at the polls and report them immediately.

Each of our reports leading up to the 2008 election have sought to empower the voter through awareness, such as checking their registration, voting early, and in this case, checking your touch screen results before you walk away from the machine.

I encourage all of you to join us at videothevote.org and become part of the citizen oversight of our elections. Help everyone get the story straight.

CHAPTER 17

In Ohio Union Vote, a Call to Video the Vote

11/07/2011

Ohioans go to the polls tomorrow to decide on SB5, a bill passed by the Ohio legislature that intends to dissolve public employee unions. This law is similar to one that was enacted in Wisconsin earlier in the year, but it goes further, to include the dissolution of firefighters and police unions. The placement of this ballot measure to be able to vote down SB5 was achieved by a referendum submitted with over 300,000 signatures. Along with a referendum on whether Ohio will recognize any national healthcare legislation, this off-year election has shaped up to be a contentious one, with significant Get Out The Vote efforts on both sides.

Besides being a perennial swing state, Ohio itself is a bellwether for the national mindset and prognosticator for political trends. The presidential election of 2004 revealed rampant breakdowns in election administration by Secretary of State J. Kenneth Blackwell, disenfranchising thousands from voting in a close election. A subsequent investigation of the House Judiciary Committee led by Rep. John Conyers reported:

"We find that there were massive and unprecedented voter irregularities and anomalies in Ohio. In many cases these irregularities were caused by intentional misconduct and illegal behavior, much of it involving Secretary of State J. Kenneth Blackwell, the co-chair of the Bush-Cheney campaign in Ohio."

In the wake of the 2004 election meltdown, concerned citizens banded together to document the 2006 national elections, using the newly-launched YouTube for real-time reporting on voter intimidation, closed polling places, misinformation, long lines, or any other problems.

The current Ohio Secretary of State, Republican John Husted, is not offering an exclusive voter hotline like his predecessor, Democrat Jennifer Brunner, but is otherwise maintaining the same procedures her office implemented when it sought to clean up the electoral process in the ensuing controversy surrounding Blackwell's tenure, according to Husted's office.

The fight over voter access has continued in Ohio, with a Voter ID bill yet to be decided, along with a redistricting map proposed by the Ohio GOP that the Ohio Democratic Party is challenging in court.

A coordinator for Video the Vote Ohio, J.R. McMillan, explains that this election year presents an opportunity to prepare for the 2012 elections, while taking stock of the fallout from the foreclosure crisis.

"Of significant concern this year is the potential for hundreds of thousands of Ohioans to be denied their right to vote as a direct result of the mortgage crisis which has had an enormous impact a state already facing 15 consecutive years of increasing foreclosures. Layoffs, work stoppages and lack of new hiring, especially in the auto industry and larger manufacturing sector, have pushed many more into home foreclosure or an unexpected move in search of steady work. One of the often unforeseen consequences of such widespread relocations is the adverse affect moving has on voter identification and eligibility."

Even those lucky enough to move from a home into an apartment in the same school district or general vicinity may be surprised to find their polling locations have changed. Many have yet to update their voter registration, something of little immediate concern for those trying to find a job or just feed their families.

Worse still, Ohioans who may be in the process of foreclosure or living with friends and family while looking for work or a place they can afford, many not have the necessary documentation to prove residency. Drivers' licenses will still have their former addresses, and those living on the kindness and compassion of others aren't likely to have a utility bill in their names.

Even with Ohio's proposed voter ID law failing to move forward in the Ohio Senate and opposed by Ohio Secretary of State Job Husted, hundreds of thousands of Ohio voters who have been forced to move since last November are at risk. As if losing their jobs and losing their homes weren't bad enough, many Ohioans will discover on Election Day that they have also lost their right to vote."

Originally based on a bucket-brigade model of dispatchers, shooters, runners, and uploaders, technology has made portable video sharing ubiquitous. Tech advances assist in learning about voting problems as they arise, as well as offer platforms for sharing reports by citizen journalists. Video the Vote Ohio will be following the efforts of organizations like Election Protection and tracking Twitter hashtags and Facebook posts for trouble reports to proactively dispatch filmmakers to problem-plagued precincts.

CHAPTER 18

This July 4th, our Elections are in a Free For All

07/03/2012

On July 4, 2011, former President Bill Clinton spoke to students in Washington for the annual convention of Campus Progress. His message to them was surprisingly stark and pulled no punches. Coming from the famed triangulator who faced impeachment from Republican lawmakers after giving them NAFTA and Glass-Steagall's repeal, this was a warning to the young audience in attendance as well as their brethren across the country inheriting the American experiment in democracy:

"I can't help thinking since we just celebrated the Fourth of July and we're supposed to be a country dedicated to liberty that one of the most pervasive political movements going on outside Washington today is the disciplined, passionate, determined effort of Republican governors and legislators to keep most of you from voting next time," Clinton said at Campus Progress's annual conference in Washington.

One year later, this assault on voter access continues full steam. From Florida Gov. Rick Scott's targeted voter purge to ongoing battles over Voter ID laws, our next presidential election could well be decided by only one state overwhelmed with voter suppression tactics.

As we have seen in 2000 in Florida and in 2004 in Ohio, a full-court press by those wishing to interfere with voters can deny the popular vote and let partisan officials decide the election for us. As we have learned since those elections, the only thing more costly to our country than two wars was the Bush tax cuts. Not only do elections have staggering consequences, the subverting of elections have even greater implications.

The identity and ideal of America is so noble to us, no matter how many bad actors we have to face from time to time. From this goodwill and principle woven into our national fabric, our high expectations of fellow Americans can leave us vulnerable to deceit. And while concerns about election integrity were once swiftly denied by both parties, overwhelming evidence of voter suppression and electoral manipulation have made election administration a new spectator sport.

In 2006 I co-founded VideoTheVote.org, a national effort to recruit volunteers to document polling place problems on Election Day and share reports via the newly-launched YouTube. From polls opening late to machine breakdowns to improper provisional balloting to misinformation to intimidation — citizen journalists nationwide shared their stories. In recent election years, the media has taken up covering polling place dramas, although they tend to gravitate to the more tabloid tales of the day (see: Ohio poll worker bites voter's nose).

For this election in 2012, live streaming technology allows Video The Vote unprecedented opportunity for real-time reporting and follow-up with election officials. A new smartphone app will bring the 866-OUR VOTE hotline into the Cloud Era. Video the Vote will be working before election day to report on voter access issues nationwide, on Election Day to report and address voting issues, and after election day to follow up on Voter ID law impacts, possible recounts, purging outcomes and more. With more and more young Americans mobilized around issues facing the 99 percent, learning The Playbook of Voter Disenfranchisement is key to fighting for your voice.

My 2008 documentary *FREE FOR ALL!* explored the Ohio 2004 election and its mismanagement by Secretary of State Ken Blackwell. From partisan maneuvers to deliberate confusion to outright deception, Ken Blackwell left no trick untried from The Playbook. I am proud of this film as a record for history reflecting the extraordinary steps taken to deny democracy, and validated by how our accuracy has borne out. (Indeed, there was more afoot in my own film than we could predict.) Roger Ebert wrote of *FREE FOR ALL!*: "The doc is engrossing, even enraging. ... [Ennis] has a lot to say."

This Fourth of July, I encourage you to watch and share this film, which begins and ends on Independence Day, and start working in your state toward a fair Election Day. And as you watch your local Fourth of July parade, remember that politicians generally don't organize parades — they show up in front of them.

I thought I couldn't do much as just some dude, until I realized that the guys running things were just some dudes as well.

CHAPTER 19

Brad Friedman:
Counting Chickens

Brad Friedman, journalist and radio host, spoke at L.A. Café, a salon of progressive activists, shortly before the 2012 presidential election.

*   *   *

FRIEDMAN: I suspect you did hear that ACORN committed voter fraud. ACORN did not commit voter fraud. Ever. There is not a single a piece of evidence showing that any fraudulent vote was ever cast due to a fraudulent registration by one of ACORN's workers. One of ACORN's workers who were turned in to authorities by ACORN themselves when they were defrauded by the small handful of ACORN workers. And yet you heard about ACORN.

You've heard about that over and over again. You've heard the lies about ACORN, and that has been in play now for years. Even before ALEC started pushing these bills, Republicans have been pushing this notion that there is massive Democratic voter fraud going on and therefore we need polling place photo ID restrictions in order to stop it.

Charlie White, the Secretary of State of Indiana, was found guilty of three voter fraud felonies this year and thrown out of office. Indiana, by the way, is the first state in the union to require photo ID restrictions at the polling place—and yet their Secretary of State committed three counts of voter fraud. He was thrown out of office earlier this year for it. He's a Republican and apparently the photo ID restrictions they had in place in Indiana did not stop the top election official in this case from actually committing voter fraud. Okay? Photo ID restrictions at the polling place are a scam. It is meant to keep people from voting, period.

A recent study came out about two or three weeks ago confirming that there are 10 known cases of in-person polling place impersonation in this country since the year 2000 in all 50 states. Ten cases. That's it. That's out of hundreds of millions of votes cast. This is a scam. The in-person polling place impersonation is the only type of voter fraud that can possibly be stopped by polling place photo ID restrictions. That's it. And yet, they are dead set on trying to keep hundreds of thousands of minorities, elderly, students, poor people from being able to cast their vote this year. It is horrible.

It is worse than just photo ID restrictions. It's ending early voting hours. It's throwing dead people off the voting rolls, who have this nasty habit of not actually being dead. Throwing non-citizens off the voting rolls who have this nasty habit of not being non-citizens.

It's really bad this year, and before anybody starts celebrating because they think Mitt Romney is self destructing, I would beg you and plead with you do not count any chickens, okay? This is bad, this is very bad, and I'm here to tell you about it.

Now one of the reasons why this is bad is the fault of progressives, is the fault of Democrats, is the fault of voting rights people. And I love Color of Change. So don't get me wrong here. I love the work Color of Change is doing, but the problem in this country, when it comes to this photo ID issue, is not voter ID. We have got to stop calling it voter ID. People hear that and they go, "Well, what's wrong with identifying yourself before you go to vote?"

This isn't a matter of framing to trick people into believing one thing or another. This is about facts. The facts are that voter ID is already required in a majority of states. It's required in all 50 states under federal law. Already, for first-time voters, if you have not registered at the headquarters of the county, you will be required to show ID when you go to vote—reasonable ID. Bank statements, paycheck stubs, driver's licenses, if you have it. There's nothing wrong with voter ID, in and of itself. The problem is, narrowly-tailored polling place photo ID restrictions: state-issued photo ID, a certain type of photo ID that they know 25 million Americans who are eligible to vote do not have. Please, I'm begging you, stop calling it voter ID, it's polling place photo ID restrictions, and it is set to kill us in state after state after state.

And when I say us, I mean us voters. Us voters. This is not about, for me, this is not about Republicans or Democrats or anybody else, they all have enough supporters, people who don't have enough supporters are the voters, and I'm standing up for them. And I'm standing up for them in states like Kansas, which President Obama probably won't win, in Tennessee, which President Obama probably won't win. I don't care. I think everybody in Kansas who is eligible to vote ought to be able to cast their vote and that's what I'm fighting for. And by the way, the Department of Justice ought to be fighting for it in Kansas, in Tennessee, in Pennsylvania, in all of these states under the Voting Rights Act where they are not currently bringing the fight. So we need to hold progressives accountable, we need to hold the administration accountable, we need to fight for voters!

Sorry. I get worked up about this, because I don't want to come back here in four years, we got to take care of this now. The fact of the matter is, if people get in to cast their vote -- if they're allowed to get in to cast their vote -- those votes still need to be counted, and counted accurately, and in a way that we can know that they have been counted accurately.

I've been speaking and thinking of Don Siegelman, former Governor of Alabama. I've been speaking to him over the last week or so because he had to go back to jail, to federal prison, last week for supposed bribery, for a crime that has never been a crime in the history of this country. I won't go deep into those details, he's a former Democratic Alabama governor, he was brought down by Karl Rove and his cronies at the Department of Justice and in the judiciary. But the reason I'm bringing him up is because in the year 2002, Don Siegelman was up for re-election. He went to bed having been announced the winner. And when he was woken up in the middle of the night, he was told that in the middle of the night, in one Republican County in Alabama, they found that over six thousand votes had been mis-allocated from him originally. They were shifted over to his opponent Bob Riley, whose campaign manager is married to the U.S. Attorney who would eventually prosecute him. And they're all clients of Karl Rove.

But what happened was his votes—and his votes only —were moved over from him to his opponent, and thus, he lost the race. This was on paper ballots, paper ballots optically-scanned with an electronic tabulator made by Diebold. But he was never allowed to count those paper ballots, he just had to trust whatever the computer said was the truth. He was never allowed to count the ballots, so we don't know if he actually won or lost that race. He believes his race was stolen from him; I tend to think he's right.

In June of this year, in Wisconsin, you might have heard there was a big election? Some recall elections. And people were again counting their chickens leading up to the election. Everybody was feeling good, it looked like Scott Walker was gonna be removed in this recall election. And when the polls closed at 8 o'clock on Tuesday night, June 5th, all of the network television, the news networks, Rachel Maddow, everybody else was saying, "This is too close to call, it's gonna be a long night, get your popcorn out, we've been following these exit polls all day long— exit polls that we, in the media, get to watch that are taken from people walking out of the polling place" (and, by the way, you don't get to look at those because you're just people, but the media gets to look at them.) And the people coming out of the polling place were saying "We're voting for Scott Walker! And, as a matter of fact, we're evening voting for President Obama!" They supported him by more than 8 percentage points.

But in the Walker race it was neck-and-neck, "It's gonna be a long night, we may not even know until morning, until dawn"…and then in about thirty minutes it was landslide: Scott Walker.

Now by the time they announced the landslide for Scott Walker, not a single paper ballot cast in Wisconsin had actually been counted by any human being. Every single result that they reported on was from an electronic computer tabulator which may or may not have been right. We don't know. But they presume it's right and they count none of them by hand afterwards. The entire country will be using these machines again on November 6th.

Now just in case you think this is crazy talk, conspiracy, there's nothing to worry about, these computers always get it right, they couldn't possibly malfunction, they couldn't possibly be manipulated, I will remind you that just two months before the June 5th election in Wisconsin, down in Palm Beach, Florida—our old friends in Palm Beach, Florida—they had municipal elections there, and three different races were announced by the computer, three different candidates who lost the race were announced to be the winners. By the same computers that were then used two months later to count the ballots in Wisconsin: Sequoia optical scan systems, a company named Sequoia, they're now owned by all one company. But, that was only found because the sharp-eyed election director in Palm Beach County, Susan Bucher, actually bothered to look at a couple of those ballots by hand, and she noticed, "Wait, we got a problem here, these people who lost were announced the winners by these computers."

Now with all of this voter suppression that's been going on this year, and all of these Republicans trying to keep people from voting—I said I was nonpartisan in these issues, I am nonpartisan, but I'm also going to call out the bad guys when they are clearly the bad guys. And the Republicans are trying to keep you progressives from being able to cast your ballot.

And all of the talk about this has obscured the concerns that we have, that I have, that you should have, about the voting system that we use in this country. And when the winners are announced on the night of November 6, please remember that we will have little or no idea if any of those winners or losers actually won or lost because we don't count ballots in this country.

I have been begging people to fight like hell for paper ballots over the years and a lot of people have finally begun to get that message, even though 1/3 of the country will still vote on 100% unverifiable touchscreen voting machines this year. But a lot of people know that we need paper ballots. But we are not done when you cast a vote on paper. Stick around, stay at the polling place, try to count those goddamn ballots, if you can! Keep your eyes on what's going on.

And then for the long term, I have been able to find nothing more secure, nothing more reliable, nothing more over seeable and transparent -- which is required for self-governance -- then hand counting paper ballots at the precinct on election night in front of all parties, all video cameras, and everybody in the public, with the results posted at the precinct before those ballots are moved anywhere. That's the solution; how we get there between now and then is about education, it's about giving the message correctly, it's about letting people know we're talking about election fraud, not voter fraud. The voters are doing fine! Please, leave them alone! (Unless they're Mitt Romney or Newt Gingrich or Thaddeus McCotter or these Republicans. We've got a voter fraud epidemic when it comes to Republicans.)

But, by and large, the voters are doing fine, please leave them alone. It's election fraud we need to worry about. And it's about getting the message out correctly. Not in way that "people can buy", but in a way that is truthful and accurate and reflects the problem we're faced with in this country. It's about the people. We've got to stand up. We've got to make noise. And we've got to make noise against the progressives and the Democrats who don't get the message out correctly. It starts here and I ask you all to join me in this effort. Thank you.

CHAPTER 20

Putting Our Country Back Together

12/04/2014

A largely quiet tactic to disenfranchise voters of all persuasions has become a target of reform-minded citizens in the wake of the 2014 midterm elections. While we have seen widespread pushback against voter suppression, unreliable voting machines, and unchecked spending in elections, gerrymandering — the process of selectively re-drawing voters' districts to ensure the outcome — has reached a critical mass in the fight for American democracy. This is a tactic favored by incumbents of either political party, and as such this is a non-partisan issue affecting the public at large.

Retired Supreme Court Justice John Paul Stevens writes in his book *Six Amendments* that we even need a new amendment to the U.S. Constitution to prevent this disenfranchisement in states across the country:

Districts represented by members of Congress, or by members of any state legislative body, shall be compact and composed of contiguous territory. The state shall have the burden of justifying any departures from this requirement by reference to neutral criteria such as natural, political, or historic boundaries or demographic changes. The interest in enhancing or preserving the political power of the party in control of the state government is not such a neutral criterion.

One of the considerations that prompted Stevens to make this recommendation was the 2013 government shutdown, which let extremists dictate the fate of the majority because their districts were safely conservative. Stevens also cites the notoriously malformed District 30 enacted in Texas in 1991, which looks like fractals on a bender.

And while some states have taken the initiative to reform their state's re-districting process, such as California's ballot-initiative success, the Supreme Court stands to decide if such citizen-helmed efforts are legal in a case coming from Arizona. Justice Antonin Scalia lamented "severe partisan gerrymanderers" in a 2004 opinion, but we'll see if he the man who believes in the devil can concur that with gerrymandering, the devil is in the details.

In Ohio, where the last election yielded all predicted winners based on their districts, even opposing activist groups joined together for a revamped redistricting process. Progress Ohio and Opportunity Ohio united as the Voice of the People Coalition in response to a report by League of Women Voters released post-midterms, which revealed how elections were essentially predetermined in Ohio due to gerrymandering.

This unlikely push from progressive organizers and a conservative think tank in turn helped spur both political parties to reach a deal on the redistricting process this week. "I am very pleased with what we have and I think this is moving forward in a way that will create much greater fairness," said Richard Gunther, a political science professor at Ohio State University who has worked with

League of Women Voters and Common Cause to improve the process. This is "vastly better than what we currently have. Both parties made significant concessions. Neither side got everything they wanted."

This is just the beginning, as we put our country back together into communities, not commodities.

Texas 30th Congressional District, 1991

CHAPTER 21

People Power Prevails at the Supreme Court

07/01/2015

At a volatile time in American democracy, where candidates by the dozens curry the favor of billionaires and citizens openly question the validity of elections, the Supreme Court this week upheld an important tool in revitalizing our democracy.

To be sure, the Roberts Court has proven to be a demolition derby for policy, where petitioners go to be bludgeoned with precedents, no matter how obtusely. In last week's historic decision on marriage equality, the dissenting justices selectively built up their own arguments against gay marriage based on plaintive prejudice, willful misreading of the case at hand, and at times open contempt for those seeking dignity and equality under the law—a surprisingly prohibitive mindset considering the words over the front of the court read, "EQUAL JUSTICE UNDER LAW." (The justices probably enter through the garage.)

Justice Antonin Scalia, once considered a vaunted scholar, has in recent years fallen in stature by his own doing, from reading his own unrelated editorials on immigration in the court, to citing cases completely wrong, to asserting Congress should not be interdicted one day while haughtily striking down an act of Congress the next.

And yet, for the justice whose vocabulary rivals Shakespeare's, Antonin Scalia will not be remembered for his judicious prowess, but for dissenting in a fit of pique: "Ask the nearest hippie." Clarence Thomas raised the bar for coldness, suggesting dignity for gay couples is not given through the law, but up to themselves, just as slaves had the choice of dignity while being considered property. This, from a man whose own marriage would have been illegal 50 years ago were it not for the Supreme Court legalized interracial marriage. Chief Justice Roberts, who has acted so proactively in the interests of corporations before, based his heartless dissent on the plainly wrong premise that humans have always considered marriage to be one man and one woman, conveniently forgetting polygamy throughout history while conveniently ignoring the question before the court, like in his hijacked adjudication of *Citizens United vs. F.E.C.*

Such detachment at the upper echelons of our constitutional system of checks and balances makes it all the more surprising when the court returns a decision advancing the rights of people over the establishment.

In *Arizona State Legislature v. Arizona Independent Redistricting Commission,* the court ruled that citizens have the authority to determine how their voting

As arcane as matters of mapping may appear, I assure you: when they say, "The devil is in the details," gerrymandering voting districts are those details.

This is why things don't change. This is why laws stay the same no matter how many kids get gunned down. This is how elected lackeys concerned with a corporate agenda more than the lives of their constituent's children stay in office. Rewriting electoral districts has become an entitlement to the party in power. Instead of governing cities, counties, and townships in an efficient reflection of population and density, redistricting has taken recalculation to obscene new lengths. With the help of computers, districts are drawn around the voters, down to the block. Instead of a map of counties clustered together, congressional districts from state to state look like a concoction of Legos spanning for miles.

Citizens have been standing up to this for years in their hometowns, and seeing people mobilized and being impactful makes others want to do something, as well. The documentary Gerrymandering is an inspiring look at how citizens and leaders came together across party lines to bring a citizens' redistricting panel to California, similar to Arizona's efforts. The people power you see in that film is a testament to the work that still stands today after this ruling by the Supreme Court. Once the California Citizens Redistricting Commission was established by ballot measure in 2008 (Prop 11), voters expanded their role in a subsequent ballot referendum in 2010 (Prop 20). These may seem like small steps, but the people are beginning to police their politicians.

And this is just a start to crack down on gerrymandering. Over-arching rules must be adopted that prohibit gaming the electoral map. Even a former Supreme Court justice believes we will need an amendment to properly remedy partisan redistricting, as John Paul Stevens writes in his book Six Amendments.

That amendment can happen. The amendment to overturn *Citizens United* will happen. Our country was not just founded on people power, it became great through people power. Suffrage was the result of people power, lowering the voting age to 18 was accomplished through people power, and we are taking back our democracy from the pay-to-play system for them, and for our grandchildren. We are not leaving our futures to be written by a few imperious bigots.

CHAPTER 22

Confronting Voter Suppression in 2016

04/29/2016

Ten years ago, when I started making an investigative documentary into what happened in the 2004 election in the deciding swing state of Ohio, I wondered what thwarting an election might look like and how I could even show such a thing, let alone make it watchable and credible.

I would end up interviewing election officials, newspaper editors, investigative reporters, authors, bloggers, activists, lawyers, professors, party leaders, statewide candidates, community organizers, lobbyists, whistleblowers, elected leaders, religious leaders, the Secretary of State of Ohio, and local voters.

I discovered no lack of evidence that the 2004 Ohio elections had been subverted; I found more damning information than I could even fit in the film. I had to learn a lot about how elections were administered to be able to comprehend the myriad of ways one can screw them up.

For instance, I found out that each of Ohio's 88 counties had its own methods of casting votes and counting them, selected from voting options provided by the Secretary of State. I came to understand that while everyone is looking at the totals on election night, efforts to undermine the election can be underway long before—and after—that night.

I was so compelled to find out what was happening at the polls in Ohio, I co-founded Video the Vote to report on voting problems on Election Day 2006. The goal then was to be able to report on any issues while the polls were open, using a new website YouTube.com, working with a bucket brigade of videographers, runners, and uploaders responding to voter hotline calls.

Whereas I had hoped just to find a few people in Ohio to help, we ended up having thousands of volunteers nationwide. Come Election Day, I was given a front row seat to election problems across Ohio and around the country: long lines, poll workers giving wrong instructions, voting machines that didn't work, polling places that didn't open on time or even have ballots, misinformation tactics, voter intimidation, purged voters, the list goes on.

We worked tirelessly to release this documentary to raise awareness during the presidential election in 2008, since it showed how the last two presidential elections were gamed in 2000 and 2004. When it was released, *FREE FOR ALL!* was well-received but met with resistance to the idea that our elections might be rigged somehow. Some didn't want to appear conspiratorial, some doubted it outright, some were worried it would discourage more from voting.

Ten years later, faith in our elections appears to be at an all time low. I see state after state confront massive electoral dysfunction, citizens unable to vote because of new state laws intended to make voting harder, along with some asserting that any election their candidate didn't win must be rigged.

In *FREE FOR ALL!* we investigate and list a staggering number of approaches to voter suppression and election theft: Biased officials, voter registration prevented, wrongfully purged voter rolls, voter intimidation, voter misinformation, confusing polling places, untrained poll works, voter ID barriers, long lines, provisional balloting, and that's all before you even get to cast your vote on what may be a touch screen voting machine unable to verify your vote was properly recorded.

I also learned that there are a lot of election officials who take their job seriously, want to be fair, and are trying to operate with equipment they have been issued by state officials who may be partisan, or may be responding to voter demand with new systems. It's the presumption of working professionally and transparently that allows partisans to run rampant given the chance to oversee themselves.

Seeing as how it took generations of struggle for this democracy, and that our right to vote is written in blood, I believe it is a fundamental responsibility to vote, and it is also our responsibility to make sure every vote is counted. Privatized election companies threaten the transparency of our vote totals if their voting machines, tabulators, and electronic poll books can't be audited due to trade secret. Boards of Elections in each county and your Secretary of State are the ones who determine vendors for election contracts.

There's a reason Diebold voting machines were abandoned in Ohio, California, and elsewhere—mobilized citizens with proof of DRE's fallibility were persistent in making the case to their elected officials and the press that touch screen voting machines were unreliable. Even skeptical journalists had to take note when the C.E.O. of Diebold promised in a letter to Bush donors that he would deliver Ohio's votes for George W. Bush.

When we started Video the Vote in 2006, we needed a video camera and a tape deck to upload a video to YouTube; today smart phones let us broadcast live worldwide immediately, but we still need to know what to look for. While there has been much attention to exit polls of late, the surveying of a small fraction of voters is a sampling aimed at finding out why a voter voted the way they did and what types of people voted for what, it's not an effort at a parallel election. If we want to rely on elections that count every vote, it seems misplaced to over-emphasize a sampling of dozens, perhaps hundreds of voters, out of hundreds of thousands of people voting.

That's not to say discrepancies in exit polling do not belie vote flipping—just that it is not logical evidence of votes being changed.

Similarly, there has been much attention to voter purges in New York, Arizona, and elsewhere following primary elections where thousands of people discovered they were not registered to vote. I observed that Maricopa County, AZ, was a hotbed of voter complaints on Super Tuesday in 2008, so the electoral meltdown this year was not surprising. A state's voter rolls do have to be purged over the years to remove dead people and old addresses, an important step in preventing voter fraud. Given the under-funded bureaucracies that administer and process local elections, it can be hard to determine if a would-be voter was not registered because of a mistaken purge, or they didn't update their voter registration with their new address, or the DMV failed to process their registration properly, which is often.

That's not to say there aren't voters purged from voting rolls with the intent to disenfranchise—Katherine Harris and Jeb Bush purged hundreds of thousands of Florida voters illegally in 2000 claiming they were felons (so we can stop blaming Ralph Nader already). In 2004, the RNC organized a massive operation to challenge voters who did not respond to certified mail, a tactic known as "caging."

But these tactics are just playing cute when it comes to passing legislation outright with the clear intent of making it harder to vote, like the restrictive voter ID laws that sprung up since the Supreme Court ruled in April 2008 to uphold Indiana's photo ID law in *Crawford vs. Marion County*. Given that the Supreme Court saw fit to gut the Voting Rights Act in June 2013 for *Shelby County vs. Holder*, the urgency of filling the vacancy on the Supreme Court can't be stressed enough, as this is an opportunity that comes once in a generation.

There is no one way our votes are at risk, and there is no one time we need to be paying attention to our local elections. Since all elections are local, you have a right from living where you are to make sure your elections are secure, your vote is verifiable by recount, and your registration is accurate. That means getting involved in the election integrity movement, beyond your candidate's campaign. This means pushing for laws that expand voting, it means refuting myths of in-person voting fraud which are used as justification for disenfranchising voters with selective photo IDs. It means learning your state's voting technologies and confirming that your voting machines are reliable. This means making sure you are registered, and like Santa's list, you are checking it twice.

We can't always tell the difference between maladministration and malfeasance when it comes to fixing our broken elections. But we can start now on making it harder to not get it right.

PART FOUR

The Obama Administration

CHAPTER 23

How Can We Trust Our Elections?

05/19/2016

When I set out to document election fraud ten years ago by traveling around Ohio with a video camera, I knew I had my work cut out for me. The suggestion that the presidential election, in America of all places, could be stolen earned you an incredulous look, if not laughter in your face. And this was from Democrats.

A lot can happen in ten years. Now many on the Left seem to readily accept any theory of election theft offered. Now the media follows voter suppression like the new electoral horserace, from following Voter ID laws that make it harder to vote, to upholding the myth of in-person voting fraud.

I've been following the news closely for more signs of voter disenfranchisement in this primary, so I was alarmed to see this headline come out the night of the Kentucky primary: "31 Kentucky Counties Report Election Fraud."

Wow! Already proven election fraud? In so many counties? I knew there were serious doubts about the last gubernatorial election in Kentucky, but this seemed major. I saw that the headline was on a blog, so I was skeptical that this wasn't paranoia posted as fact. But no, it was from the local news, WSAZ, even the same headline.

The Kentucky Attorney General's election hotline received 76 calls, about a range of voter concerns: A voting machine question, a couple of procedural questions, a concern about an election official, confusion with an absentee ballot, someone electioneering within 100 feet of polls.

These were ordinary election day issues, far from election fraud. In fact, having done my share of Election Protection work, this sounds like a pretty quiet day. I remember on Election Day in Kentucky 2006, there was a fistfight at a polling location, but for curiously non-partisan reasons: a poll worker told a voter they had to vote for the judges, but the voter didn't want to because they didn't know anything about the judges on the ballot (usually the case), yet still the poll worker was adamant about completing the ballot, and it came to blows. In Cleveland on Election Day 2012, a disagreement outside a polling place between two people resulted in an election monitor approaching to resolve the dispute, but BITING one of the people on the face before running away, ultimately getting arrested. This was the person there to resolve disputes. Still, even face-biting isn't election fraud.

Getting terms right and being accurate while making charges of election-meddling matter. In 2006, I had to accumulate copious proof to show people that it happens. In 2016, that standard of proof still matters, even if it is a notion we can now discuss. Right now, Baltimore is reviewing its most recent election after state officials decertified the primary results amid striking irregularities, such as a thousand more votes cast than voters who checked in at the polls.

It is that kind of statistical deviation that is an alarm. While much has been made of trusting exit polls lately, the reality is, the veracity of exit polls in U.S. elections has been greatly diminished since the 2004 election, when exit polls showed John Kerry beating George W. Bush in Ohio and other states, only to see those states go to Bush. Despite the mountains of voter suppression and evidence of manipulation that would pile up about the 2004 election, pundits and journalists joked long after about exit polls' unreliability, diminishing the credibility of such polling in the mainstream media and in the minds of voters. In *FREE FOR ALL!*, we show how divergent exit polling was an indicator in the 2004 election, and we also show how reporters were quick to blame exit polls for being wrong immediately after, including Dan Rather.

Exit polling results used to be reported while the polls were still open, but that practice was discontinued so as to not dissuade people from voting if they thought their candidate would lose or was safe. Similarly, at some point since 2004, the folks that conduct exit polling stopped trying to keep their own count of votes as an indicator, and focused more on how different population trends voted. Now, exit polling firm Edison Research makes no claims about trying to approximate the vote count in its research— you can read their explanation on their website.

I would prefer to know that there is a "back-up" headcount going on at polling places, like a canary in a coal mine, to give a heads-up when something seems foul. But these are news organizations paying for this, an atrophying industry, which is why exit polls aren't even done in all the states. Our voting system, like it or not, is still the best way we have to count everybody.

That's one of the reasons I want to continue the movement to Video The Vote. Ten years ago, myself and fellow organizers tried out this new website that had launched called YouTube.com, which allowed one to upload video files free of charge for other people to watch on the internet. Shooting video at that time involved a non-HD video camera recording onto a small DV tape, perhaps a memory stick, and then capturing that video on a computer to upload it to YouTube where it would be viewable, in a couple of hours.

[To some people, reading that last paragraph might seem like what it took to make wax and dip candles so that settlers could see indoors at night with candlelight.]

A lot can happen in ten years. Today, we have mobile apps in our pockets that broadcast live worldwide in HD with geo-tagging and a cloud backup. Instead of watching social media to find out what is happening at the polls, we can go to our polling places and report for ourselves what is going on there.

Because ultimately, we need to be able to show others that these problems exist, and the people we need to convince to make reforms aren't just going to take our word for it.

CHAPTER 24

Obama's Coup in Cairo

7/10/2009

For all of the analysis, parsing, and knee-jerking from Obama's address to the Muslim world, there was one detail that seemed to bypass the pundits.

Obama acknowledged the U.S. role in the 1953 coup of Iran, when the CIA worked to overthrow a democratically-elected secular leader, Mohammad Mossadegh. This isn't fringe conspiracy theory, this is a widely known history (not so much stateside). And it is an all-time chart-topper on "Why They Hate Us."

In 1951, after British oil interests refused to pay Iran an equal share of their revenues, Mossadegh nationalized the oil industry and took back the reins to his country. After embargoes and blockades against Iran failed to return oil control to the British, Kermit Roosevelt, Jr., grandson of President Theodore Roosevelt and employee of the Central Intelligence Agency, devised a new approach: Operation Ajax. Through bribes and bargains, locals staged scenes posing as dissidents and malcontents, while the media would be used to stir Mossadegh's ousting. While Mossadegh would die in confinement, the autocratic and oil-friendly Shah Mohammed Reza Pahlavi was restored to power.

Until the 1979 Revolution. Iran's leader being installed by foreign interests never sat well with the Iranians. As such, the theocratic radicals held a nationalist high ground when Ayatollah Kohmeni took over the government. And as long as I was old enough to remember after that, Iran seemed scary.

This is an example of how short-sighted greedy goals end up causing long-term world problems. If Iran was not alienated from Western nations, how different would our geo-political world look today?

Obama's acknowledgment was not an apology: "In the middle of the Cold War, the United States played a role in the overthrow of a democratically-elected Iranian government." This suggests that not only is Obama aware of what the CIA has done in Iran, but other countries since.

In the best-selling memoir, *Confessions of an Economic Hit Man*, John Perkins details his career of predatory lending to Third World governments on behalf of American-backed businesses. The example of Mossadegh proved particularly persuasive to leaders unsure about opening up their country to U.S. industries. Perkins and others have more to say on skullduggery in the name of empire than myself — even Kermit Roosevelt, Jr., wrote a book in 1979 about how he did it, Countercoup: The Struggle for the Control of Iran. But there is presently a powerful parallel at play in Peru:

Villagers in the Amazon have long been exploited by oil companies that pollute their land, violate agreements, and harm the locals. The new president of Peru, popular with the petrol peeps, wants to open up to 60% of his country for oil drilling and logging. As the local issues throughout the jungles have been ignored, villagers have organized, demonstrated and stopped work at the oil refineries. Their strike is being fought by the police, who have been having deadly clashes with thousands of protesters and villagers over the last week. These people were suffering in a different jungle than the one where some jerk on a reality show was complaining about his fame being devalued.

Obama is the first president to acknowledge the U.S. subversion of a democratically-elected Iranian government, but he can still do better. Hegemony has left many scars around the world, and Peru is just one of them. Obama may not be able to foil a game as old as empire, but as President he can — and should — do something to help stop the bloodshed and refinery strikes in Peru.

CHAPTER 25

Picking on Pelosi

06/26/2009

It's no secret that the Republican Party is struggling. Polls show party membership at a low of 21%, the crazies have scared off the credible, and the leading spokespeople are beauty pageant runner ups. The languishing magazine business is even piling it on, suggesting that morbid fascination in the wane of the GOP goes beyond the blogosphere and Op-Ed pages, and is actually tabloid-worthy.

Thus, Republicans continue to assert their irrelevance through the concerted effort to act like it is suddenly so clearly necessary that Nancy Pelosi resign as Speaker of the House. After all, she said the CIA didn't divulge all of their interrogation tactics seven years ago, and how could anyone question anything the CIA said?

John Boehner, Newt Gingrich, Mike Huckabee, Steve King, Dick Morris, Sean Hannity, and others aggressively defending the CIA look disingenuous. We don't really believe that they believe that this secretive bureaucratic goon squad is honest about its activities and intelligence. Honestly, they probably get off on the idea.

Defending the CIA against accusations of lying or unseemly behavior is quixotic. It's like acting indignant in defending the mores of Motley Crüe. To recount some of the Central Intelligence Agency's greatest hits makes it sound like Cobra from G.I. Joe, the venerable cartoon black ops army with no actual ideological agenda other than evil (before Blackwater). The scheme to sell cocaine to make money to fund a rebel army on the other side of the world was hatched by the CIA, who then lied about it to some guy we arguably elected President, John Kerry. The CIA is the Machiavelli of government agencies.

As with so much in the wars of partisan rhetoric, these arguers are more steadfast to dispute any point making their side look bad, because they fear that their entire ideology fails with it. These Bush apologists were happy to accept that a baseless war was the fault of bad intelligence from the CIA like it was all just a case of food poisoning.

No, the Right Wing readiness to ignore criticism of the CIA and pounce on Pelosi really reveals their pervasive, peculiar, and apparently perverted obsession with Madame Speaker. From the beginning of her tenure as Speaker of the House, Pelosi has been demonized by Republican rabble-rousers to rattle their base. Her San Francisco sensibility was supposed to be code to the bigot belt, that she would spearhead some homo agenda, and maybe make Congressmen hold hands and share their feelings. Pelosi's outsized political persona has more to do with the paranoia prodded by poor punditry than her stalwart stewardship.

It's reminiscent of how vilified Hillary Clinton was as First Lady, when she was still rocking spray bangs and shoulder pads, doing photo-ops with one billion children. But the threat loomed, Republicans sneered, that this pushy dame had a mind of her own, and might just try to get into the act some day. Of course, they were all right about that Hillary Rodham — she revealed her own ambitions, and damn near went the distance, with even Ann Coulter cheering her on.

I had the opportunity to see Nancy Pelosi speak at a *Politco* panel in Denver during the DNC last year. She explained in so many words that as Speaker, her job is to get things through the House that can pass. Say what you will about her politics — Pelosi has shown herself to be shrewd and prudent, aware of her attention, but downplaying her presence.

As such, her effort to distance herself from the CIA's conceit on torture should not be surprising or cause for outrage. To presume the benefit of the doubt with the CIA after countless destroyed interrogation tapes doesn't even pass the straight face test. Whatever discussions Nancy Pelosi ever had with intelligence officials about "harsh interrogation tactics" were well after these tactics were outlined intricately by Bush's cabinet. This is feigned outrage about information that Nancy Pelosi got third hand.

I suspect time will tell of the deep-seeded S&M appetites that ran through the minds of Bush's neo-con perv party. Psychoanalysts will write books on how cabinet members held top-secret White House meetings to conspire about getting men naked and bent over to submit to their throbbing power. Those meetings got detailed in order to hand down the specific language to the CIA. Was anything ever acted out as well? You know, just to explain the positions?

Is it so hard to imagine Donald Rumsfeld snapping his fingers at some poor Pentagon aide to get down on all fours on the carpet as a "visual aid" in front of a stately Colin Powell and a vaguely aroused Dick Cheney? Now, in the middle of that tableau, comes the cold-water question that is bound to ruin the mood: "What do we tell Nancy?"

126

Cut to a much graver briefing with pretentious security presence as Rep. Pelosi is slid a very legit-looking file folder, with a cool CIA watermark and shit, and some bullet points in Courier font and spiffy legalese about how seriously we are going to get those bad guys. Pelosi, not yet the Speaker or third in line for the presidency or the most powerful woman in the history of the republic, nods solemnly at the grim assessment, appreciative that they tell her anything.

And now, after so much hot air and regurgitated half-assed talking points, it has come down to powerfully plain sexism: Did the RNC really release a video comparing Nancy Pelosi to Pussy Galore from Goldfinger? (They did.)

The irony is that in the movie Goldfinger, Pussy Galore was the rare exception of a Bond girl who saved 007's ass when his suave plan fell to crap, and she alerted the CIA to save the day. Besides provoking a unifying growl from women who normally wouldn't care about Nancy Pelosi, the RNC has unwittingly crowned her the most popular Bond Girl of all time, beating out Grace Jones. Nice!

But the restless right-wing attacks, as ridiculous as their rhetoric may be, must continue to be debunked and discredited. They can seem scatter-shot and trivial now, but it was after years of an unchecked, open-ended investigation through Bill Clinton's entire career and associates that a popular president was impeached for off-topic lying about his sexual exploits. Controlling the debate and confronting misinformation is akin to justice, and similarly demands eternal vigilance.

CHAPTER 26

When Karl Rove Squeals, You're Doing Something Right

10/13/2010

In the wake of recent revelations about foreign spending on U.S. elections, President Obama has called out the Chamber of Commerce for its anonymous donors toward campaign ads in a series of speeches over the weekend. Karl Rove has at once made uncharacteristically desperate efforts to deflect this from becoming an issue in the home stretch of the midterm elections. As Shakespeare observed in Hamlet, "Methinks the lady doth protest too much."

When Obama took to the campaign trail for the long weekend last Thursday, the news had spread from *ThinkProgress*'s report on the U.S. Chamber of Commerce receiving money from foreign donors. Obama intoned to a crowd in Chicago: "Right here in Illinois, in this Senate race, two groups funded and advised by Karl Rove have outspent the Democratic Party two-to-one in an attempt to beat Alexi — two-to-one. Funded and advised by Karl Rove."

Karl Rove went to the last refuge of the scoundrel, Politico, and was quick to change the subject with a non-denial bringing up talking points about the stimulus and healthcare reform.

Obama continued in Maryland, as reported by ABC White House correspondent Jake Tapper: "Just this week, we learned that one of the largest groups paying for these ads regularly takes in money from foreign corporations."

The president then took this step, saying, "groups that receive foreign money are spending huge sums to influence American elections, and they won't tell you where the money for their ads come from."

Obama kept it up in Philadelphia, as reported by the *Washington Post*:

'The American people deserve to know who is trying to sway their elections' and raised the possibility that foreigners could be funding his opponents.

'You don't know,' Obama said at the rally for Senate candidate Joe Sestak and other Democrats. 'It could be the oil industry. It could even be foreign-owned corporations. You don't know because they don't have to disclose.'

Sunday morning, Karl was blistering with outrage and indignation on, of course, FOX News, as reported by Sam Stein on the *Huffington Post*:

'They are tossing out these baseless charges,' said Rove. 'The president of the United States accused the Chamber of Commerce, and the Democratic National Committee in its new ad accuses Ed Gillespie and I of a criminal violation of our law by getting foreign money and spending it on American political campaigns, and they have not one shred of evidence to back up that baseless lie. This is a desperate and I think disturbing trend by the president of the United States to tar his political adversaries with some kind of enemies list, with being unrestrained by any facts or evidence whatsoever.'

'Have these people no shame?' he bellowed later. 'Does the president of the United States have such little regard for the office he holds that he goes out there and makes these kind of baseless charges against his political enemies? This is just beyond the pale. How dare the president do this?'

How dare he, indeed. How dare Obama point out the obvious inequity of campaign spending this year, now with Republicans outspending Democrats 7-1. How dare the president of the United States voice concern over foreign influence of America through anonymous cash windfalls, and at least request to know the identity of the big spenders. "Have they no shame?" Like Rove has endured humiliation McCarthy-style before the House of Un-American Activities Committee, his persecution has been unfathomable, and we should feel for him. (Like, say, Don Siegelman).

And leave it to Rove to be able to evoke Nixon's "enemies list" idea, having worked as Young Republican Chair on Nixon's campaign. As David Corn observes, questioning the intent of major donors who wish to attack candidates while hiding in anonymity is hardly an enemies list. Of course, the notion of "baseless charges," is telling, when no real charges against him have been made — yet.

Rove puts on a show as if he has somehow been wronged because he knows that once he's tainted as the guy overrun with corporate money from only the most sinister industries, the money people won't risk getting associated with him. Rove probably is genuinely surprised, because Democrats never attack the corporate money giants, instead hoping to get even a portion of the table scraps that the elephants keep getting. But I think after Republicans have outspent Democrats 7 to 1 this year, the donkeys were bound to kick.

Worse than that, it blows his narrative into the crack smoke that it is: when real people are losing their homes, he is raking in tens of millions of dollars to advertise to those people to vote for the banks, brokers, and lobbyists who helped take their home from them. That's a hard enough job for Turd Blossom to spin for his party with a straight face, even on FOX News via satellite from his closet, no wonder he is so despondent. And no wonder FOX news quickly reported it as if Obama was "scaling back" his criticism after Rove's rebuke.

That Rove even emerges to put an immediate spin on something is striking. Look at like this: Have any of us heard a peep from Dick Cheney since the BP oil spill, which was brought on in part by shoddy Halliburton cement well casings? Funny how he is not on FOX News threatening us all with terrorism so close to the election. George W. Bush is not the most popular ticket in town, if people could still afford tickets to things.

As much as he has tried to pretend he hasn't ruined countless lives posing as a go-to shill for FOX News in recent years, it's not like Karl Rove is someone people really rally around. He's not even really popular with Republicans or conservatives, because they probably sense that even though he's fighting for their team, he probably does not give a flake about their beliefs or principals. Even they know he's disingenuous when he talks, but they appreciate the always-lofty talking points. But he's not, say, a Sarah Palin, that some people will really want to relate to and project themselves onto no matter what stupid thing they say. In fact, he's the consummate Washington insider that Tea Partiers think they are revolting against. No one really wants to be Karl Rove, except other aspiring shady political strategist/sociopaths. So Rove didn't really have to wail on TV like a Real Housewife unless he was perhaps A) protecting business to reassure backers, or B) emotional and jumping the gun out of guilt, or C) a combination thereof.

Rove isn't in this for power anymore. Not personal beliefs, political ideology, even money. While he is certainly motivated by ego, that's not why he is desperate. No matter what he says, no matter how cold any investigation went, Karl Rove knows that he could wake up tomorrow to a press release about a hearing from John Conyers or Al Franken about something that could be the beginning of the end for him. Rove knows what deals he cut with Patrick Fitzgerald to squeak by the Plame grand jury. Rove knows about the ongoing court case King Lincoln Bronzeville vs. Blackwell about the dramatic events in Ohio surrounding the 2004 elections, culminating in the untimely death of a close associate of Rove's who was being deposed in the case, Mike Connell.

Karl Rove needs GOP control of the Justice Department so that he can wrap up loose ends and not have to keep looking over his shoulder. Rove is always looking ahead, and will be all the more anxious if there is a chance that his plans will be denied.

And, I think, there's another reason Rove is nervous about the public attention turning toward these anonymous attack ads. Once people start to distrust the ads on TV, an effective tool to sway people has become blunted. Rove knows that once Americans stop buying whatever scare tactic he is flashing in front of them, it will require more work to suppress the vote —like caging, which he pioneered as a form of knocking voters off the registration rolls, an evolution of the computerized voter tracking systems he developed under the Nixon years, as I detailed in my film Free For All!

The Patriot Act was a product of Karl Rove, because he convinced Americans they were disloyal if they did not consent to relinquishing many of the rights guaranteed to us for centuries in the Bill of Rights. Though in all likelihood used by Rove more to spy on political enemies than domestic enemies, citizens across the continent have been subjected to warrantless wiretapping by the NSA. Millions of citizens' banking transactions were reviewed in the name of fighting terrorism, and succeeded in netting a governor in socks. Americans were arbitrarily added to no-fly lists, including a Rove biographer.

Americans surrendered their privacy at Karl Rove's behest. Karl Rove ought to be able to confirm he has nothing to hide, like the rest of Americans have had to in the public interest. The IRS has already been asked to look into the donors, and surely Mr. Rove would want to allay Americans that he is not taking foreign money to run ads attacking government officials. Karl Rove should identify his funders for American Crossroads and Crossroads GPS. How dare he do this. Has he no shame?

CHAPTER 27

The Monkey, The Organ Grinder, and The Swift Boating of Van Jones

11/10/2009

It's kind of like the organ grinder and the monkey. The guy with the music box gets the monkey to dance and act out for the people. And when huge corporations, media interests, and high-priced consultants unleash desperate distortions on public policy, they get a robust jig and a squeal from right wing reactionaries, hot heads, bigots, and people who don't know enough to know they don't know enough.

The problem is, the Media, and apparently some in the Obama Administration, listen to the monkey.

Van Jones has made an abrupt and indignant departure over an empty outrage, letting Obama sacrifice talent and control of the debate in one reflex. While Jones may well prove more effective on the outside of the tepid D.C. mechanisms, that his departure was prompted by Glenn Beck hysterics sends the misleading message that Glenn Beck actually matters. Regrettably, resignation signifies an acknowledgment of impropriety. The right wing parrots refer to it as a scandal, but nothing has actually happened.

This manufactured Van Jones controversy was alternately marketed as "What is this Czar title, anyway, and why is a Russian king ruling our government? That's Communist!" Lost on the clap-traps might be that the title of czar dates back to Nixon and was popularized by Reagan. These are the embittered and disaffected looking to argue over anything, constructing justification for their displaced anger, as opposed to looking for truth.

The other non-troversy came in a speech where Jones referred to Republicans as "assholes" in the way they successfully managed to pass legislation. He also suggested he could be an asshole, i.e., effective. Though this was meant as the same observational truth as in "the assholes always get the girls," it was seized upon like red meat by jackals. No matter if the Vice President can tell a Senator to go fuck himself on the floor of the Senate without rebuke, or the fact that overreacting and feigning outrage to try to get a guy fired really is kind of an asshole thing to do. Jones has so far failed at living up to this, and makes a lousy asshole, and will probably not be scoring with the cheerleaders, some of which he certainly could have used for the past month.

The other tacked-on outrage was that Van Jones had signed a petition supporting further investigation of 9/11. A petition demanding truth about 9/11 is hardly a controversy, and it shouldn't be. As The Dude (Jeff Bridges) yells at Walter (John Goodman) in *The Big Lebowski*: "What does anything have to do with Vietnam?!" The same could be said today about 9/11, to Truthers, to Freepers, to Rudy Giuliani. This point is not even debated, it's like Van Jones knows the profile of harassment. If it's not this, it will be something else. Is your vehicle registered? Are these headlights up to code? Is that brake light dimmer than the other one?

Of course, there is more to this abrupt umbrage about Van Jones than some petition or profanity. As Adele M. Stan details at AlterNet, Van Jones is a threat because of the entrenched industrial opposition against green jobs. Noticeably, this attack on Jones has been unrelated to Van Jones actual performance, obscuring that Jones was at the White House to create millions of jobs in the midst of recession.

Predictably, the right wing chatterbox has crowed over Van Jones's departure, as surprised as anyone that their complaining has actually resulted in anything. This is a Pyrrhic victory, delighting trolls who get to write "HA!" and "I'm driving my low MPG truck to show Van Jones." This Administration — at least the few progressives within it not driven to placate business interests — is trying to offer health care and environmental conservation not just for all Americans today, but for generations of Americans to come. This costly din and derision of partisan patricide is far more destructive than foreign enemies.

There is another irony lost on the harpies so quick to clamor for accountability for things real or imagined, from the past, present, or future. The very point of public office is that the public can demand accountability. Government officials are ultimately responsible to the public.

On the other hand, private companies can do whatever they want, as long as their shareholders are happy. And they can lie. They can say their product does not kill people when they know it does. And they can keep that vital information confidential under trade secret protections, endangering the public. And individual executives are almost universally unaccountable in corporate crime. Vioxx. Monsanto. Enron. Goldman Sachs. Philip Morris. Etc.

Despite considerably more attention and infamy, does Erik Prince step down from Blackwater (Xe), particularly now that he has been implicated in the murder of potential whistle-blowers? Erik Prince would tell you to go his idea of a Christian Medieval hell, he owns all of Blackwater, he inherited his millions to go play war games, and no one can figure out what court in the world to even try his crimes in. Till then, he will keep getting new contracts with the U.S. State Department.

Corporations only answer to government when government demands it. Unfortunately, the demanding is usually done by politicians who have to run for re-election and could always use some more contributors. In light of the Supreme Court mulling over corporate monies into our elections, I believe we are approaching a new debate on campaign reform that will expose more people to how beholden our elected officials are.

Thus, this is another circumstance where the ranting righties who have crusaded against any government role in anything presume that same transparency and entitlement that they would be denying themselves in every other role of society, and doing it self-righteously. That you even have a right to call for his resignation proves the main advantage to administration by elected officials.

These are the same people who get inflamed that the President of our country would offer a broadcast message to welcome students back to school. Fears were repeated and escalated that Obama would indoctrinate all children into socialism if they were exposed to even minutes of hearing him speak, like he isn't on TV every day already. Something that could be motivating to children who do not subscribe to a two party mindset was politicized to preposterous ends by people desperate for credibility while devoid of ideas.

If you are afraid that your child will abandon all that you hold sacred after a couple minutes of a grown up explaining something about government on a TV, then you have no freaking control over your kid anyway, and probably never will.

Personally, if this is a public education that I am paying for with my tax dollars, I for one would like a celebrity cameo from the government to show some effort, a little pizazz, like a fancy in-flight video.

These people are scaring their kids with made up ideas of Obama, and they don't know what he would say because they never even listen to him. They don't have to listen to anything, they know they don't trust him, because they have heard so much about what a socialist he is, and even though they don't know what that means, it must be bad, because the white people on FOX keep yelling and crying about it. And the kids grow up thinking the same thing without questioning, and the disconnect proliferates.

This cuts to the heart of the problems we face in instituting such basic government services as health care and sustainable development. When there is so much disinformation — literally, one of the biggest industries in America is mass-producing mistruths and distortions, and it is owned by Rupert Murdoch — there will thrive a chronic disconnect in society.

Where the Obama team was the Marketer of the Year in 2008, this year they have less marketing muscle than the crude new Melrose Place. Obama mistakenly believed that upon entering the White House, people would listen to him just because he was president, or something. No matter how well Jackie Robinson played, he had to face the cruelest critics the most often. Obama is still the subject of prejudiced suspicion, both racial and cultural, but amplified to near mythic proportions of being a Marxist dictator, without having done anything (almost literally) at all.

The Big Tent is a fallacy, and there will never be any participation from a dedicated segment of society that is committed to vitriol and tearing down that tent at all costs.

This deference to disapproval, acquiescence to any angry and aimless mob, it is far more respect and legitimacy than they would return in kind at the sign of offense. These are people who for the most part hide behind screen names while demanding to personally inspect the long form documentation of our President's birth, so that they can find other reasons to complain either way.

This is the base that Van Jones is worried about distracting from health care reform? We need to draw their fire. Van should blare the new Jay-Z on the Front Lawn of the White House while planting acorns to freak out the Ditto heads while the grown ups meet inside and stop posturing over talking points, like their lowest denominator is watching. The rabble-rousers will rabble on, regardless.

To that end, perhaps what is needed is to offer fodder to inflate the self-preoccupation of that right-wing shark-osphere.

Where the signs typically say, "Do Not Toss Items to the Monkey," this is where to start. Feed the monkey peanuts, cotton candy, popcorn to gobble down. Throw it gossip, confusing riddles, internal strife, distraction. Give them more chew toys to tire themselves out with. Wave shiny things in front of their wide, eager eyes. Delude them with relevancy and mock them as the alienated, small-minded, insecure, intolerant sociopaths that they are. We need rope, lots of it, to let them hang themselves in their xenophobic obsessions.

Because what won't deter them is shame. There is no shame to these hacks like Glenn Beck, Newt Gingrich, Sarah Palin, John Boehner, Tom DeLay, and their cadre. Beyond cultural bias, this is an automatic opposition to anything that could be successful. Seeking to earn the approval or inclusion of this deluded minority is ruinous. It offers easy exploitation from predatory industries that have long proven their disregard for American citizens in the interest of profits.

CHAPTER 28

How Rahm Bombed

10/06/2010

In a Rockwell-ian retrospective softening of Rahm Emmanuel in the *New York Times*, David Brooks relates his personal experiences of a kinder, gentler Rahm, one that does not cuss or bully others into submission, as Rahm is regularly described as, even by President Obama. That the only fond thoughts on Rahm's departure are coming from a conservative Beltway columnist reveals the inefficacy of Rahm as Chief of Staff under the first two years of Obama.

It is tempting to oversimplify Rahm's impact on the Obama Administration as a short-sighted bully who may well have screwed what could have been a great presidency with his belligerence to cover up his lack of political acumen. So let me dispense with the platitudes and give in to temptation.

Where Karl Rove was "The Architect," Rahm was more like the shady Chicago contractor you can't get on the phone. I admonish Rahm because I am sick of bullies, especially ones that stand in the way of work getting done while they flail about abrasively. He chose to intimidate those around him and the base he could take for granted, avoided fights with those provoking a fight, and cut favorable deals for the ones he should have been fighting.

I do not begrudge Rahm his lack of progressive alignment, as many have. Rahm's well-known contempt for the liberal base that catapulted him into the White House reveals not just a deep disassociation with Middle Class America, but a glaring indication that no matter how loudly he swears, he doesn't understand how shit works.

When told that progressive groups were considering running ads for a more progressive candidate in a Democratic primary, Rahm called them "f-king retarded!" When Sarah Palin demanded that Obama fire Rahm and managed to make the subject about her, while Rahm had to acquiesce into some special-needs charity gestures. Rahm really should have been required to work for the progressive groups he was cursing out — collecting signatures on the street, having to listen to others' ideas, and not having anyone from Big Money give a crap about you.

Rahm's wrath was on display after the fierce primary earlier this year in Arkansas for the Democratic nomination for the Senate seat held by Blanche Lincoln. Bill Halter drew widespread support from progressives and unions to unseat the blue dog Democrat, but incumbents tend to work for other incumbents. The night of Lincoln's narrow win, a statement smacking of Rahm was issued from the White House: "Organized labor just flushed $10 million of their members' money down the toilet on a pointless exercise." In Pennsylvania, when the progressive-backed Joe Sestak won the Democratic primary and retired the White House-backed Sen. Arlen Specter, despite Rahm"s dissuasion via Bill Clinton, those campaign dollars apparently did not go to waste.

It's not that I am so outraged like Michael Moore that Rahm is so contemptuous of the progressive base of his own party, he would flippantly interject "Fuck the UAW" in a bailout meeting, dismissing the middle class families that comprise it because they lack clout. But I would think Rahm might at least consider the opportunity of appealing to the votes of unemployed auto-workers — they are going to vote for something that improves their situation. Or, you could blow them off and ponder the swelling ranks of the Tea Party.

While famously barbed in his meetings and deal making, it is apparent that Rahm simply doesn't deal with people or issues he doesn't want to deal with. Perhaps it is rationalized as go-it-alone or defining new priorities, or showing people up by touting disregard to try to make them feel small. But Rahm's shoddy record of tenure reveals how small time he really is. Our country languishes today in atrophy from pay to play politics. Rahm is just another player in this, but more like a coach for the neighborhood bar's softball team, not a Yankee.

Here is the simple truth: Rahm was never thinking about voters. He was thinking about donors. Campaign money means more than votes in his old school mind, so as long as the big donors were getting heard, those liberal losers with websites were just going to have to suck it up and still vote Democratic, because there is no other option.

And so in the course of financial and health care overhaul, concessions were made to giants in insurance, pharmaceutical, banking, and brokerage, after unprecedented bailouts to the financial industry. Even David Brooks alludes to this in his one critique of Rahm: "He made some big mistakes: Trying to use the financial crisis as an opportunity to do everything at once." Interesting way of putting it — 'doing' it for whom?

Come election season, shocker: Republicans are getting more money than Democrats at almost 6 to 1. Karl

Rove is sitting on a $50 million dollar slush fund of anonymous cash. Was Rahm actually expecting gratitude, even deference, compared to the party that lives only to de-regulate big businesses? From these titans of greed? Rahm's savoir-faire is like expecting flowers from the frat guy that told you he had a girlfriend before he date-raped you.

The Rubin-esque financial team assembled under Obama will all be at the Goldman Sachs Holiday Party this year, I have no doubt. And they'll all be talking about the prospects for business under a well-worn madam like John Boehner as Speaker of the House. The House Minority leader is so shameless, he will keep asking Twitter where the jobs are, while voting to support China's currency manipulations that deprive jobs in both countries. John Boehner is so shameless he will keep demanding the deficit be reduced first and foremost while in the same breath insisting on extending Bush's generous tax cuts for the rich that will add billions more to the deficit.

In his gushing NYT column today, Brooks cooed, "Rahm is completely in touch with his affections and aversions. He knows who and what he loves — Obama, Nancy Pelosi" If he loves her, then why hasn't he helped her stay House Majority Leader? Pelosi in the end is the one that revived the over-compromised health care bill to pass at all. And on the New York Times website, just opposite David Brooks yearbook note to Rahmbo, is Bob Herbert bemoaning the audacity of John Boehner's tidal wave of money and self-aggrandizement.

Rahm has lost to John Boehner on both counts: He can't possibly hope to be more shameless an advocate for the rich and win their donations, and he also couldn't call out a buffoon like Boehner and demonize this guy who spends a third of his year on a golf course. Where the rest of the Republican Party has acquiesced to the far right fanfare about gay Kenyan abortions, Boehner has left himself as the Bill O'Reilly of the GOP, spewing out the same hollow talking points from 2003. At the recent Pledge to America unveiling, Boehner admitted, "we are not going to be any different than we've been," to lay-ups by Stewart and Colbert. And this guy is up to be third in line for the Presidency. Again, like under Bush.

The Obama Administration could have dispatched with Boehner so long ago as the bronzed poster boy for corporate cash while not dignifying the nascent Tea Party rabble with direct criticism, but rather re-directing it at the party responsible for the economy. By acting like Obama was automatically too big for any of this kept his team's biggest player on the bench.

The Obama Administration's silence in response to right-wing hysteria has been deafening. While an overarching character trait of Obama's is to maintain composure in the face of racial hysteria — which tends to be lurking at the bottom of much of the Tea Party — that does not mean that the best thing to do is ignore the outspoken opposition.

The Rise of the Fringe

Obviously you can't control what your opponents want to think about you when they are coming up with anything that sounds bad, even if they don't know what it means. Republicans have taken to blatantly wishing bad things to happen to America so that they can get into office, rather than have to come up with a good reason that they should lead. And Rahm can't be held responsible for the brazen bias of FOX News and News Corp, which has finally dropped all pretenses and started giving millions to Republicans outright.

But the very mindset of having to sell everything to the Beltway, that is the tragic flaw that Rahm brought with him to a leader who literally had both houses of Congress and a laundry list of reforms ready. A master of the House of Representatives who oversaw new candidates into the fold, Rahm advised the President to let Health Care and other policy initiatives run their course through Congress, rather than seem overly reform-minded and getting in front of these important changes he was marshaling into a desperate America (behavior known to some as "leading").

The carnival atmosphere that has ensued from the fringes of conservatism has been a self-propelling reality show fostered by a corporate media that cares more about getting some crazy on camera than acknowledging issues that actually affect way more people.

Republicans, along with the conservative and mainstream news (nary a difference these days) were outraged that Stephen Colbert testified about migrant farm workers and legalization of undocumented workers. Despite the fact that Colbert has done more to support our troops than they have, or even acknowledge the painful truth that Colbert brought to Congress and the public, these commentators spent a week condemning the very testimony as a stunt and an affront.

This from the party whose own U.S. Representative took to the floor of the House of Republicans to debate provisions of health care legislation presenting a baby. Rep. John Shadegg (R) of Arizona explained that this baby — not even his, just somebody"s baby — apparently knew that health care reform, while good intentioned, was not properly funded, and socialist. While this could have been tied to an amendment lowering of the age to be an elected official to 6 months old, this really was empty showmanship, and should have been called out as the lamest political stunt since the last time John Boehner openly wept.

But even if he was dismissing the increasingly desperate right wing agitprop, there were less-profile, though more crucial responsibilities of Chief of Staff that Rahm neglected as well.

The Justice Department

As detailed in Harpers, one of the primary responsibilities of a Chief of Staff is to fill court vacancies, and by that measure Rahm was a total failure. Scott Horton writes that this "points to a White House that is simply oblivious to the nominations process. On this measure, Rahm Emanuel is the worst performing White House chief of staff in recent memory." Again, this missed opportunity may enrage progressives, but I am struck by the lack of practical forethought.

Inheriting a Justice Department that had been widely known to be forged at the pleasure of Karl Rove, Harriet Miers, and Alberto Gonzales, not only did the incoming Obama Administration not relieve and rehire US Attorneys as is its right, they let the ongoing US attorney dismissals investigation close abruptly with dubious reasoning.

If there is a Republican majority in the House, I have plain expectations that there will be impeachment proceedings against Barack Hussein Obama. For anything. Allegations of smoking in the White House, a non-smoking public building. Hearings for Obama's birth certificate—

not just to prove he was born in America, but to prove he is over 35. Shameless hacks like John Boehner would rather take thousands every day from lobbyists while repeating rhetorical questions in tears, rather than let attention drift to how little the GOP has to offer, or that Boehner is out every evening early making the rounds at DC bars.

A Justice Department that is at best impartial if not disloyal would have staved off whatever cockamamie investigations are sure to come on taxpayer money from blowhard Representatives wielding anonymous babies. A Justice Department that was doing its job would be drawing the line at torture and stopping the illegal imprisonment at Gitmo. And a shrewd Chief of Staff that looked toward the next election (like Karl Rove) would use the Justice Department as the voting rights cops they are supposed to be used, and stop the Republican games of voter suppression from caging that keep coming up every election cycle.

Over at the Justice Department, maybe Attorney General Eric Holder never had the portraits of George Bush taken down, since he seems confused whose administration's laws he is enforcing. But Rahm knew who his boss was. Rahm didn't have to clean up the Justice Department because it would have thrilled progressives, or to encourage actual law enforcement and impartiality, but I would think this would happen from the interest of self-preservation alone. It's like one of the most important courses required to graduate, and Rahm never even showed up for it.

Ironically, this slide down the hustlers' totem pole for Rahm was precipitated by the failed Chicago bid for the 2016 Summer Olympics.

The Chicago Way

A classic Sean Connery movie line written by Chicago playwright David Mamet is delivered in the film The Untouchables: "He pulls a knife you pull a gun, he sends one of yours to the hospital you send one of his to the morgue. That's the Chicago way!" Rahm's approach seems as corny, and indicative of how short sighted and destructive his tenure as President Obama's Chief of Staff has been. (On this gruffness, Brooks waxes: "He's managed to preserve the patois of Chicago, the earthy freneticism of his Augie March upbringing.")

Rahm's power play may well not have transpired as we see today had Chicago got to host the 2016 games, instead of the humiliation of early elimination by the International Olympic Committee, who ultimately decided to give it to the Vegas of Violent Crime, Rio. (Have you seen the shocking Sundance documentary Mada Bala (Send a Bullet)? Yeah, apparently neither has the IOC. Chicago should have just bought the IOC a copy.)

Chicago was so broke, it made the ill-advised deal to privatize all of the city's parking meters to some company for $1 billion cash upfront. The deal is for over 75 years, three generations of Chicagoans. Talk about mortgaging your children's future, and for ultimately so little. As Chicagoans exploded over the jacked up costs of street parking, that billion dollars is going to start to look like $26 worth of beads to buy Manhattan.

So the Daley Machine spent whatever money it could get to woo the IOC and advertise the 2016 games like they were already happening ($76 million in the end). Even Perry Farrell had to pander onstage at Lollapalooza (from the mainstage — not the Chicago 2016 stage). This is in spite of the fact that other U.S. cities have made clear their lack of windfalls in hosting the Olympic Games in recent years. While locally not a very popular cause in Chicago and logistically unrealistic (MotherF@#K YOU Dan-Ryan Expressway Interchange) Mayor Daley sunk everything on it as his ticket to payoff the massive debt Chicago was in.

When Daley saw that the wheel of fate hadn't landed on his roulette color, and watched what was left of Chicago's cash outlook get scooped away, he knew he was toast. It didn't matter that Richard Daley had been Mayor for two decades and built his own parallel political machine throughout the wards like the Cheney White House built an in-house military intelligence staff to leave the Pentagon out of the loop. It didn't matter that by now either his name or his father's name was inscribed on every piece of Chicago's stunning architectural skyline. Not only had Daley gambled and lost, he got Rahm to get the Big Man himself to personally pitch their time-share Power Point presentation.

It is doubtful that Obama would have gone to Copenhagen were it not at Rahm's behest. And that Obama did go all the way there and failed to seal the deal was allowed to be a point of unrestrained glee among conservatives in an alarming parade of spite. A week later, when Obama won the Nobel Peace Prize and would be going back to Copenhagen, those same conservatives were even more vitriolic in their spite. Where the White House was sensitive and downplayed these things, it should have capitalized on the explicit ill-will wished upon our country by the Republican Party, who are never tired of questioning people's patriotism.

Again: I really don't care about the Olympics or whatever backroom pipe dreams got cooked up in Chicago. I don't care if Obama shows up in an Uncle Sam hat to represent our country on the world stage, and I don't care if the world stage isn't buying from him, since America tends to have the Olympics here like Andrew Lloyd Weber revivals. But you don't need to apologize for winning the Nobel Peace Prize.

In the end, I suspect Rahm was being eased out of the bus, and Daley's vulnerability provided the face-saving opportunity. I wonder if Richard M. Daley heard from Rahm himself, or through an intermediary, that his reign of one-party rule was suddenly coming to an end, because somebody was looking for a new job, one that could possibly sound like a step up from the White House. Daley's abrupt announcement that he would not be re-seeking election (and the absence of any damning Blago-type scandal surfacing afterward showing he had to bail) seemed so tinny and insincere — as did Rahm's "surprise" that Daley was stepping down when he had no need to.

Feeling Rahm-orse

If Rahm's smarts had been questioned, worse still, his effectiveness was called out.

Looking to bolster his rep in the Beltway, Rahm made a plain effort at his own spin in a Washington Post column by Dana Milbank on February 21st. The curious talking-point buffet was immediately called out throughout the media as an unsubtle attempt at self-promotion by Rahm. It was then I first saw the description of Rahm as the "Mayberry Machiavelli." Even David Brooks agrees: "Over all, Rahm is a warmhearted Machiavellian." Karl Rove cooked up a sprawling media roll-out for a non-existent threat in Iraq, and we still have 50,000 troops there. Rahm tried to gin himself some good buzz and it couldn't even survive a news cycle.

Even in aiming small, Rahm has relied on blunt insistence, while preferring to ignore other matters of obvious priority. Worse still, he probably thought he was brilliant for it. Why Howard Dean was shut out of the White House after leading the DNC to a new surge probably has to do with Rahm, whom he had worked closely with in the 2006 50-State strategy. Now that Republicans are employing the same strategy this election cycle, I wonder if putting up with Howard Dean's pomposity was such an obstacle to retaining power.

But the only real problem with Rahm is that Obama has listened to him. Obama has joked about Rahm's intemperate management and made it seem okay because it was effective. Roasting Rahm while still in the Senate, Obama quipped that as a teenager working at a deli, Rahm lost the top of his middle finger in an accident, rendering him practically mute. This made Rahm being a well-known jerk apparently okay.

"Entourage" was Obama's favorite show on the campaign trail, and this has been widely covered, as has the similarities between Jeremy Piven's manic bullying character and the Emanuel brothers. The parallels were intriguing — the glamorized insulation of widely loved celebrity among his friends who had his back, with a pit bull of an agent whose abusive means are charmingly justified by the ends. But at some point, I think Obama grasped the shortcomings in Rahm compared to the macho alter-ego of Rahm's brother Ari on "Entourage."

On that show, *deus ex machina* runs rampant, in a soapy fantasy life kind of thrill. *Deus ex machina* is a term from Greek drama referring to when a god was introduced to the stage—a crane that would lower an actor from the top of the stage who was wearing a mask that projected their voice, who would make a pronouncement of a sudden change of fortunes for the characters, by the gods' decree. In storytelling, when a convenient windfall or extraneous gift is given to a character rather than their having worked and built up to it within the story, that kind of easy-writing device is known as *deus ex machina*. To go from obscurity to president so quickly, Obama must be able to relate to the experience of *deus ex machina*. And while "Entourage" isn't Ayn Rand unrealistic, I fear it affected Obama's perception of how good of a job macho Rahmbo was doing.

This isn't lamenting "Entourage"; that's the point of the show — to keep seeing how life gets better for these guys in spite of themselves, and we enjoy watching it because that shit doesn't happen to us. That is what entertainment is for. Even its star Adrian Grenier gets this and made a documentary about it. But I never thought such a wish fulfillment bro-medy could be so dangerous (to grown men with law degrees, anyway).

And so it is with dim hopes that I watch Rahm wade back into the swamps of Windy City politics. It is troubling to know that Chicagoans will be subjected to a resurrected version of the Daley Machine, like another vaguely recognizable Terminator spin-off. Maybe Obama will be himself now; maybe he will dress down his opponents like he does so well when allowed to acknowledge them. And maybe the President will recall that voters got him there, along with a lot of small donations. At least today, I have no doubt there is celebration among employees in the West Wing. I can only hope they are able to spread their new found freedom to the rest of the country.

CHAPTER 29

Why Mitt Romney Won't Get the Job

02/06/2012

The 2012 campaign may have already reached an apex of agape anticipation at what Mitt Romney is about to subject himself to.

In an economy run into the ground by Bush's $2 trillion tax cuts, after the unrelenting arrogance of Speaker John Boehner's sole recovery strategy to continually tweet "Where are the jobs?" he has an answer: about 2 million more of them in the last six months, according to the latest jobs report.

It gets worse for the corporate raider that made mountains of money from firing people at other companies. The most talked about moment from the Super Bowl today is not Madonna or Manning but Clint Eastwood, and his Oscar-winning skills waxing a thank you from Detroit to Obama for keeping the auto industry (and its jobs) alive. So stirring and inspiring was this Republican filmmaker's ode to Obama that Karl Rove, the master of anonymous attack ads and Super PAC media saturation, scoffed that he was offended by the Chrysler spot. Clint Eastwood and Halftime in America were trending the next morning on Twitter over anything else Super Bowl related, including the hash tag "#SuperBowl."

It's bad enough that Romney has to make repeated remarks about how weirded out he is about poor people. His handlers know that just looks bad, but it's not like they're losing any poor people's votes.

But the reason Team Romney is walking off a pier in concrete wingtips is because his campaign represents the most clueless padded elite, at a time when most Americans are so desperate, they are devoid of the "fall back" mentality of automatically forgetting recent history, blaming whoever is in power and voting for the default alternative.

In the wake of Romney's resurgence after the South Carolina primary, much attention was paid to the boost he received from his debate performance, where he embraced an angrier tone, imitating Newt Gingrich's successful indignant white man outrage. Too much attention was apparently paid to Romney's debate coach, Brett O'Donnell, because he was dumped from the campaign after receiving media recognition, according to Politico. Romney staffers chaffed at the credit, and O'Donnell was not invited on to continue with the campaign as had been expected. Romney himself wanted to be emphatic that he could come up with his own comeback, not anyone else.

And here is the abject failure of leadership in not just Mitt Romney, but of the interests he represents, the vultures who prey on society under self-righteous claims of capitalism, but whose innovation is the exploitation of their workers. Whereas free markets purportedly offer a justice and balance to the universe akin to karma itself, and successful ideas are rewarded with elevation, here we see the same shark-like, short-sighted sensibility that is the real Mitt: Where someone succeeds at their job, rather than reward, they are fired, so that Mitt can reap their rewards. At a time when people are struggling for jobs and being shoved the tired Republican tripe of letting rich people keep more money as a solution to your own problems, Mitt Romney is firing the one guy doing his job well, because he's viewed as a threat. Anti-competitive practices are how he rolls. Romney and the rich giants influencing our legislation didn't get rich by competing on an open market with a level playing field. They got rich by takeovers and consolidating their competition so that they can monopolize.

Here's the problem with Romney: even Republicans don't want to vote for Romney. Many conservatives hate Obama based on conjecture or manufactured misinformation or basic policy difference. But they know why they dislike Romney. He oozes insincerity as he seeks to empathize with the struggles of the nearly half of America that is near or below the poverty line. Inherent partisan diversions won't work in his favor. Mitt Romney lacks something in common with pretty much everyone else in America: what it's like to look for a job.

It was epitomized in the moment where Romney was campaigning last year and spoke to a Florida unemployed man and commiserated that he, too, was also unemployed. Romney's tin-eared joke about his own presidential aspirations to a representative of the millions of struggling Americans kind of says it all about what he's in this for. Romney's only offering over the other Republican candidates for president is that he can speak without specs of spittle flying from a frothy rage venting at immigrants, Muslims, or debate questioners. That, and his quarter billion dollars taxed at half what you pay on your income.

All of this is not to assure Obama this is his to play safe, down the middle. If one has ever had an opportunity to lead in American history, if there has ever been a president with the wind to his back and his foes flinching in their petulant obstruction, that time is now. Obama knows what Romney will learn, that you don't get to be president by default.

CHAPTER 30

Mr. President, It's Our Moment of Truth

03/04/2015

Dear Mr. President,

From the heartlands of America to our city centers, there are too many folks who don't believe our system works. When citizens are under-served by their leaders, an apathy is fostered that enables corruption and prevents accountability. Despite the historic struggle to vote, the dream of democratic elections is at risk when the public does not take voting seriously. In cities, states and at the national level, campaigns have become a cynical game that shuns voters, and lets those with millions to spare dominate the debate and decide who runs. This has to change.

I have been inspired by the people I have met across the country who are working hard in their community to limit the influence of money in politics. They have told me in one way or another how they came to realize that until we reform how money is spent in elections, we can't confront the biggest problems facing us. And while the Supreme Court continues to disdain campaign finance regulation, the populist movement that has grown in response to the *Citizens United* decision has enacted some form of response to that decision in nearly all 50 states. There still needs to be a national remedy, and while you have voiced support for a constitutional amendment, there is a singular action that you can take right now to help restore public faith in elections and combat corrosive influences.

While Congress remains intractable over the most basic duties, it does not change the fact that our time is running out. From our environment to our infrastructure, from the care for our elderly to the education of our children, decisive action is needed to pull the curtain back on election spending. Americans have a right to see for themselves which contractors are getting paid with their tax dollars — and if those tax dollars are going back into political spending. Americans deserve a moment of truth.

We need an executive order requiring federal contractors to disclose their political spending. This step toward reducing dark money in our democracy is an important move to empower citizens, to let folks learn and be able to inform others. Elections are supposed to be a debate over the truth, yet too often it becomes about the loudest message. At least allow citizens the opportunity to look behind that message.

I am a father adding my voice to over 50 groups that have joined together to stress the urgency of this executive order, all non-partisan advocates for fair elections and civic engagement. Let Americans see if their democracy is being abused to return favors. Let the money that is driving the debate be subject to debate itself.

For too long, campaigns have been a spectacle that turns off most of the country from voting. If we are to continue the vision that our forefathers set forth as an alternative to oligarchy, it demands eternal vigilance. We can end the Pay to Play System. But now is the time to act.

CHAPTER 31

President Obama is Right: It's Time For Mandatory Voting

03/29/15

Today at the Cleveland City Club, President Obama suggested mandatory voting as a solution to the influence of big money in politics. "We shouldn't be making it harder to vote, we should be making it easier to vote," President Obama said to applause. "In Australia, other countries, there's mandatory voting." President Obama became the first president to propose this. He continued:

"It would be transformative if everybody voted. That would counteract money more than anything. If everyone voted, it would completely change the political map in this country. Because the people who tend not to vote are young, they're lower income, they're skewed more heavily towards immigrant groups and minority groups. And, you know, there are often the folks who are scratching and climbing to get in to the middle class, and they're working hard. There's a reason why some folks try to keep them away from the polls, we want to get them into the polls. So that might be a better strategy, in the short term," [Referring to the time it takes to pass a constitutional amendment.]

161

The Beltway press was quick to overreact, from the reliably reactionary *Washington Times* first suggesting the President's remarks were a policy proposal, then claiming Obama retreated from the notion amid backlash. The backlash that *The Washington Times* cites as the reason we could never have the same participatory democracy as Australia, Brazil, and other countries? Marco Rubio "noting the decision to skip an election is a form of free speech protected by the First Amendment."

Matching this determined lack of thought with diligent overthought, *The Washington Post* already re-drew the 2012 election results with what the turnout would be if voting had been mandatory. They are able to make this prediction based on more of the same people voting, for instance, matching race with the exit polls and assuming that everyone else of that race and gender would vote.

Actually, mandatory voting would be the beginning of the end of racial polarization as a means for turnout. Once our elections are not being decided by extremists driven by single issues, our elected leaders will reflect the American people.

Citizens of countries that require voting have explained to me that while their leaders are still prone to embarrass themselves, they are far closer to the middle ground than in America. Only in Congress can the refusal to do your job be a safe path to keeping your job. If we have leaders so openly colluding against our government's functionality and diplomacy, it is critical to ask how we can regain control of our country from those that would do it such harm.

I have been accustomed to confronting misperceptions about what this civic role would involve. It is striking how fiercely people will argue for the right to not vote after all that has been sacrificed for the right to vote in the first place. The foremost alarmed reaction to the idea of required voting is that it would somehow be "anti-democratic" or un-free for the government to make people participate in elections. Think about this for a moment: participating in elections, being undemocratic? The words "elections" and "undemocratic" are virtual antonyms. Yes, you can write in a candidate or cartoon character if you don't support the names on the ballot. But it is not un-free or un-democratic to involve the entire country in decisions that affect the entire country. This is how we regulate democracy. American democracy is already anemic from low participation and big money interests, with a Princeton study determining the US is now in reality an oligarchy. It is time Americans decide the future of America, not the richest with money to burn on anonymous political ads.

Is it that crazy for the government to require you vote? Isn't it a much bigger ask for the government to tell you to drop what you are doing, you are now going to war, and you'll probably die over some political B.S. that doesn't affect you? The U.S. government can issue a draft whenever it wants, and there are many who would be with us today if they hadn't made that sacrifice that our country asked of them. Does voting still seem so much to ask, especially when it can decided literally who lives or dies among us? (Did I mention you can vote by mail?)

Would it be crazier still if the government made you pay them thousands of dollars every year? What if it were in the Constitution that you had to show up at a courthouse to be on a jury? Is it totalitarian if the government made you buy your own auto insurance? Or your own health insurance?

The reality is that we are already spending a fortune in tax dollars on administering elections that two-thirds of the public are not showing up for. It is only cost-effective. Moreover, those concerned about in-person "voter fraud" should welcome compulsory voting—no more need to worry about if someone voted or not, because they all had to already. Verification is as easy as it is confirming you paid your taxes. This would make it harder for others to impersonate another voter, while offering an expected total. From there, the concern of voting experts would be on chain of custody and accurate counting of votes, something that is in the non-partisan interest of every American.

There are two types of people in our country — those that want everyone's voice to count, and those that don't. I believe that when the U.S. embraces compulsory voting, it will be the beginning of fulfilling the potential of the American experiment in democracy. Thank you, Mr. President, for wanting every American's voice to count.

PART FIVE

Rise of the Right

CHAPTER 32

What Right Wing Threat?

07/12/2009

Right-wing threats in America? Hasn't the media jumped the gun, or shark, so to speak?

James W. Von Brunn wasn't shooting at Jews at the Holocaust Museum because he was anti-Semitic. He was there to try to shoot the actual Holocaust, under the mistaken impression he could stop it still and make up for all the white supremacist mumbo-jumbo he's been known for. The Holocaust started it; this was simply self-defense.

Scott P. Roeder, who gunned down a doctor in his church on a Sunday morning, killing George Tiller after years of personal derision from Bill O'Reilly? He was not there because he was a homicidal maniac obsessed about offing Tiller and winning right-wing approval. He was just hunting. In a church. During Sunday services. Though there were no animals technically present, the stray shot might have knocked late-term abortion instruments out of the doctor's hands while he was passing the collection plate.

When Richard Poplawski was firing his AK-47 at cops in Pittsburgh, he was only trying to impress them with his knowledge of guns, sort of like a fraternity hazing. He was wearing the bullet-proof vest to impress them and make the cops like him, so they would make him an honorary deputy and give him a job. All of Poplawski's rants about Zionist control of the country and Obama's determination to take away his guns and rights, it was just water-cooler talk. Except instead of casually catching up on anti-Semitic, anti-government chit chat around the water cooler, Poplawski was commenting on Stormfront, the biggest white power web site.

The Department of Homeland Security, founded after 9/11 to provide a heads-up on dangerous threats on American soil, recently issued some kind of report or some crap, because government agencies are like that. That report mentioned something about some far-right nuts likely to act out in 2009 and do dangerous things against the government, Jews, and abortion providers. Whatever. That report was just trying to smear the shining conservative movement, and make it easier for illegal immigrants to sneak in to our country and take our jobs at GM.

Or...maybe the DHS report actually was talking about these kinds of lone nuts that we actually have to worry about, in any state across the country. Maybe conservatives and Republicans who rush to attack a security report from the government should reconsider their knee-jerk ownership of the issues and tactics that they rush to defend.

Maybe continually over-simplifying every issue in politics into a siege upon America actually helps bring about a siege mentality in Americans. Perhaps dwelling in the continual context of an election, wherein everything is good for one side or bad for the other, is really simpleminded and stupid, and creates false choices and fallacious imperatives.

And, maybe in attacking a government threat assessment, these right-wing pundits are not just aligning themselves with dangerous supremacist kooks, but even encouraging their impulses, by draping their tattered flag around those that would be singled out for wanting to go kill people they disagree with.

Bill O'Reilly, after his continual on-air assaults against George Tiller contributed to Tiller's actual assault, defiantly went on TV and proclaimed himself a victim of the liberal media for covering what O'Reilly had been saying all along. This lack of accountability in bullies and blowhards is not really surprising, and it furthers a victim branding being desperately pursued by O'Reilly, Glenn Beck, Alex Jones, that long-haired douchebag guy on Fox Business Channel, and others.

Our country was founded on revolutionaries, so apparently acting oppressed is the fallback moral high ground. This is a curious acknowledgment and embrace of the polemics from the Left dating back to the Civil Rights Era. At some point, the legitimacy that the Right denied attributing to disenfranchised groups like gays, poor people, minorities, and women in this country became the conservative rallying cry.

We see this in the vitriolic attacks alleging prejudice against Sonia Sotomayer, from old white guys who are experts on racism. And make no mistake: the more Newt Gingrich proclaims that white people are being dethroned and Dick Cheney insists humans only respond to brutality, the more these otherwise lone nuts don't feel so lonely, and believe that they have to take some kind of violent action against, oh, anybody.

I expect that these blowhards will cry out about gun rights and the threat of FEMA camps against the coming tide of rational questions, such as, "Why is it so easy for whacko fuck-ups to get an assault rifle or six?"

In a sense, these commando cowards are doing the work of scores of progressive activists, making their leaders and causes utterly repellent to the rest of the country.

UPDATE: This piece seems to have struck a chord with people who identify with the aforementioned right wing extremist nut jobs, so I think I will just apologize to all of them now and get that out of the way.

CHAPTER 33

I'm Sorry, Right Wing Extremists

07/13/2009

When I wrote my piece "What Right Wing Threat?" I might have anticipated some humorless criticism from an offended individual, outraged that I might diminish yesterday's shooting at the Holocaust Museum by joking: "He was there to try to shoot the actual Holocaust...the Holocaust started it; this was simply self-defense."

The response I got was not a diatribe from PC police, but people apparently offended by my dissing right wing fanatics. And these weren't snarky comments posted in all caps. These people called my production company. One guy with a Southern accent said something about reaping what I sow. Another woman was outraged that this senile old man who had a senior incident like shooting up the Holocaust Museum was being all exploited by the media. (My poor assistant had to politely field these calls, tying up our phone lines for all those backers who would normally be calling to give us money to produce more social documentaries.)

In my attempt to draw mainstream Republicans and conservatives away from attacking DHS intelligence reports with a partisan mindset, I figured the stark contrast from white supremacist whack jobs would be some welcome middle ground in the debate. I apparently neglected to pause and consider the feelings of the right wing nut jobs.

I would not expect right wing extremists to read the *Huffington Post*, or that they would bother with me. The piece did not really report anything new, or offer a celebrity nipple. I'm hardly part of the TV punditry circuit (though I am available).

I am further struck that this piece would be the one to draw personalized reactions. I've authored other things I would expect to be more offensive or controversial: I made light of the Rick Warren hysteria, I engaged a Sarah Palin zealot, I pontificated on how messed up Ayn Rand was, I made a documentary detailing systematic racial voter suppression by the Republican Party and showing how Ohio was subverted in the 2004 election.

But now I apparently have crossed the line by mocking the right wing nut jobs. After repeatedly stressing the differences between mainstream Republicans and conservative thinkers with racist vigilantes, I did not anticipate a spirited defense of the racist vigilantes. I kind of thought that the shooting spree thing did not need elaboration about being bad.

So I'll just skip the debate and make this a quick shout-out to the right wing extremists: I'm sorry. You're right. About everything. My bad. Pay me no mind. Go call your congressmen instead of calling me. I don't even care if you have guns, as long as no crimes ever happen with them.

Besides, the white people angry about defending the power of the white race in this country tend not to be the white people who are actually in power.

CHAPTER 34

On Teabags and Douchebags

05/16/2009

The Tea Party movement appears to be a dart board of broad complaints about American government today, insidiously co-opted by the Republican party, FOX News and corporate lobbyists.

It's like the venerable blog, "Hot Chicks with Douchebags," devoted to otherwise attractive females attaching themselves to appalling macho cheese. The mantra of the site is, "What is she doing with him?"

Somewhere in the Tea Party outrage are some desperate people asking worthwhile questions you can relate to, such as "Where the fuck is all this government bailout money going to?" and "How come I am so broke?" But before you can answer, you see they are standing next to other people who advocate burning books about evolution.

I believe this Astroturf agitprop will soon spin out, as its poorly disguised populist pitch has been revealed to be another partisan stunt with no actual criticism or legs. Just as the real Boston Tea Party involved colonists dressed as Indians to avoid retribution, this Tea Party appears to be right-wing hit men posing as concerned citizens to stage outrage.

But is it really composed of aimless, bitter conservatives chomping to criticize anything and everything that happens as long as Obama is in the White House? There is a real surge in public mistrust of the government, though I suspect much of it is based on self-propagating misinformation. Like commenters on conservative sites such as the aptly named Hot Air, one of whom said, "Obama wants to take away our rights." (Where were they for the last eight years when their rights were already taken away?)

Gone are the simplistic Good vs. Evil dogmas of the Cold War, the War on Terror, the War on Iraq, the last presidential campaign, the Wild West, you name it. Without the certainty of fighting something so easily dubbed evil, too many people fall adrift of their sense of self — what makes them good? When there is no imminent evil threat, the same paranoia finds new outlets. And so they unearth some other arcane fear-fed meme, as relevant as the Red Scare, and peddle facile orthodox with a new spectrum of threats.

And now, as an incipient extension of all these misapplied ideas of individual manifest destiny, there is the Tea Party Movement.

Like lofty literature, tying yourself to something great does not equate you as great, or even accurate. Further, simply using the term "taxation" does not imply moral superiority just because it was a word used by the founding fathers.

What is mystifying is the lack of either real policy criticism or advancement of any ideas. What is the purpose of this organized effort? A clip from FOX News: "We're hopefully going to have more tea parties...let other people know we can't believe what's going on...We're going to stand up...show the politicians...tell them how you feel...what can we do?"

It is amazing to see a movement take off without either a specific cause or a specific goal. The Tea Party movement makes a mockery of the true struggle our founding fathers fought. What they did was seriously dangerous and rebellious, an act of war with fear of death.

Today, when outrage does not take hold of the country the way some conservatives and business interests would like, the rallying cry is broadened from "cap and trade agreements restrict coal plants unfairly" to "they will take away your freedoms, guns, and children!"

Why would people think this could even be possible? Might it be because of the constant threat of socialism after every commercial break?

The outcry against socialism is in response to some imagined threat of totalitarianism that has not been raised by anyone except these outraged individuals. Naturally, that fear spreads quickly by rhetorical repetition. Those repeating these threats are the ones that have to gain by public fear.

But there is a much larger issue at stake. We need to reclaim the meaning of our founding fathers.

It is bad enough that people who haven't seen *Sex and the City* insist on waving their tea bags in people's faces. But this misappropriated sense of superiority in imitating the founding fathers leads to all kinds of wrong, like the inane videos put out by a guy in a wig on a green screen dressed like a tour guide from Colonial Village calling himself Thomas Paine.

That he is talking about something completely different than Thomas Paine writing about separating from

England is apparently irrelevant. All he needs to do is start off rhetorical questions with "Is it common sense to...?" And from there, the escalation into outright xenophobia is swift. He ends with "Buy a gun, you'll need it."

You might prefer to write off such nuts, but Bob Basso's rants have received millions of views on YouTube. Maybe some of these people really do want to go back to what our country was founded on: slavery. ("If Barack Obama could still count as three-fifths of a person, would we have to listen to him?")

While there is much prefabricated fanfare for these Tea Parties, I would caution that they are catching on with something in people right now. But here's the rub: we're stuck with them. Like the founding fathers said, all Americans have their right to free speech. And these are still Americans, who still have to be won over as much as possible. Like hot chicks with douchebags, we embrace these embarrassments, even if while cringing. That's what this country was supposed to be about: tolerance.

CHAPTER 35

Entrapping ACORN

11/23/2009

ACORN, an umbrella organization of community groups that serves poor people in major cities across the country through housing, legal advocacy, family services, and higher wages, has lost all federal funding, after decades of working for low-income, disadvantaged Americans.

That the House of Representatives has moved swiftly on anything is stunning in and of itself. More stunning, this is in response to a single independent report by conservative activists, with no follow-up investigation, no hearings, not even being provided a copy of the full, unedited video tapes shot by conservative activists James O'Keefe and Hannah Giles at a couple of ACORN offices.

This is serious stuff here. This is not a game of gotcha, of cheap political points, of practical jokes — not when this is money that helps in many real ways in impoverished communities around our country.

It is vital to assess how this backlash was accepted so quickly in light of videos that were from someone whose films are funded by conservative backers, videos that misrepresented ACORN through editing and not disclosing other failed attempts at their desired response, which may well have been dubbed over, if O'Keefe would dare to release the unedited tapes in their real context to prove otherwise.

A significant reason that this ACORN backlash has moved through Congress like Montezuma's Revenge is that this particular hidden camera stunt had the ring of "child prostitution" in it, which most politicians of either party would run from rather than dispute its irrelevance. "Anyone defending ACORN is for child prostitution" is an immediate fallacious meme. It's not like we're talking about the Catholic Church here, who still gets federal funding.

Noteworthy is that there have not been any previous allegations between child prostitution and ACORN. In this weekend's *LA Times*, O"Keefe himself asserts that this ruse had nothing to do with prostitution, importing underage sex workers, or tax help for starting up a business.

"Politicians are getting elected single-handedly due to this organization," he said. "No one was holding this organization accountable. No one in the media is putting pressure on them. We wanted to do a stunt and see what we could find."

That's what this is really about: the elections, and the threat that has been hyped tirelessly that ACORN is in some way stealing your vote.

Before I digress into the long campaign to smear ACORN because of its successful voter registration, I don't want to be accused of changing the subject to the elections. O'Keefe clearly stated that is what these stunts were about from the beginning.

There is much to dispute in O'Keefe's quote. There is no evidence whatsoever that politicians are getting elected "single-handedly" by ACORN, and it is a wild exaggeration. Many claims of voter fraud are made, few instances ever occur.

What has been distorted is that these allegations surround voter registrations, not actual votes, and that ACORN has regularly flagged forms that were incomplete, duplicate, or unverifiable. By law, anyone collecting voter registration forms has to turn in all that are used, even if they know the forms will not be processed.

Far-fetched is the idea that no one in the media has been putting pressure on ACORN. That O'Keefe would even think ACORN could elect politicians single-handedly is because of FOX News' rampant coverage and conflation of ACORN conspiracies and allegations, to the extent that John McCain worked it into his stump speech by the end of the 2008 presidential election.

The red herring of voter fraud as an excuse to deny others the right to vote is a well-worn claim. Voter suppression, specifically using the fear of "voter fraud" to advance voter suppression, is a topic I have explored and documented in-depth in my documentary Free For All! which you can see online for free right now. I also produced a video about ACORN with Video the Vote focusing on the fraud of voter fraud.

David Iglesias, a Republican U.S. Prosecutor for New Mexico, investigated allegations of voter fraud throughout the state at the urging of Republican leaders, and when he found no evidence and would not prosecute falsely, he was fired, as asserted by David Iglesias in his testimony before Congress and emails recently declassified from Karl Rove.

But again, I don't want to be accused of dodging the issue — I am just looking to rebut the persistent falsehood which directly affected this kid's motivation to punk a community organization into losing millions of dollars to help the poor.

179

O'Keefe is comparable to the FBI informant who brought down the Bronx terrorist plot — only that there would not have been any actual plot were it not for this FBI informant actively recruiting mentally challenged Muslims from mosques for this plot, which apparently involved entrapping people who were dumb enough to listen to him.

O'Keefe could well have actually attempted to show something about ACORN's voting registration controversies — by speaking to registrants who admitted falsifying voter registration forms, or following up on who registered and who voted, or even interviewing ACORN directly. But none of those would have involved a minister's daughter dressing slutty, so you can't really blame him.

So it came to pass that in this effort to dispute voter registration that Giles and O'Keefe conceived of the worst sounding scandal they could invoke, and traveled the country to ACORN offices across the country to find someone to take their time to humor them in the improv game of "Yes, And."

And they eventually found some clueless ACORN employees, people far too eager to offer good customer service than employ any common sense. A couple of workers comply with O'Keefe's outlandish inquiry for underage brothels in dispensing tax advice.

The well-publicized clips are shocking enough, and have been exploited as much as any couple of minutes of video can be. Glenn Beck taunted other networks for not covering it. Even Jon Stewart bunted on it, as if his guest interview were Sistah Souljah. As a potent testament to Stewart's "Most Trusted Newsman" gatekeeper status, the House next day voted to cut all federal funding for ACORN.

It is worth noting here that what transpired on O'Keefe's videotape were conversations about hypothetical situations — not actual prostitution, no actual crime, and not proof of an agency-wide policy or program involving prostitution or illegal immigrants. In fact, O'Keefe's experiment proves this — that several other ACORN offices would not be ensnared by their absurd scenario, and turned away these provocateurs. One office in Philadelphia filed a police report because they were alarmed by the pair.

Ironically, the only thing illegal in some of these tapes is that O'Keefe is filming illegally. States like California and Maryland have strict consent laws about surreptitious recording, which is why the news and entertainment industries have long figured out workarounds for hidden cameras. (Hint: Vegas.)

As the crankosphere raves over how the Media didn't uncover this, it is worth pointing out that not only are the tactics against the standard of journalism, the lack of disclosure and misrepresentation pushes this expose well out of the range of journalism and in to the realm of entrapment.

As it was, O'Keefe had to misrepresent a conversation where a woman stated up front that their inquiry was illegal, but played along because she figured it was a gag. Another misrepresentation by FOX was the breathless uproar about a woman who joked that she had killed her husband — well after it was established that her husband was alive, Glenn Beck, Sean Hannity, and others kept repeating the ridiculous claim for another day, demanding an investigation, since they obviously didn't have the resources as a major news network to confirm that this guy was alive.

Nor is this O'Keefe's first foray into being the Tucker Max of conservative hacks. He pulled a stunt on Planned Parenthood entrapping receptionists and donation reps into conversations where he said he wanted to kill off black people, while his compatriot Lila Rose called and claimed to be underage to see if the clinics would report statutory rape. (Lila Rose just recently called for abortions to be held in public squares to create the mass gross-out that would therefore make them all illegal.)

In a detailed response from Bertha Lewis and Steven Kest :

O'Keefe has a sordid history of preying on receptionists and other front-line service workers for respected organizations. In 2008 he pulled a similar stunt on Planned Parenthood when he and another female colleague secretly recorded phone conversations with staff who handle fundraising calls at a few of the organization's affiliates. During the calls, O'Keefe pretended to be interested in setting up funds for low-income women in need of health care. Once the conversation hit a comfortable stride, O'Keefe would change his tune and explain, in explicit language, that his real intent was to target women of color in an effort to control minority populations. The audio recordings were edited in an attempt to make it appear that Planned Parenthood was complicit in accepting donations for racist purposes. O'Keefe's intent then, as it is now, was to entrap an organization whose mission he is ideologically opposed to, and masquerade his efforts as investigative journalism rather than the propaganda videos they are.

And in college, O'Keefe showed women their place with his video wit, as reported by Media Matters:

As a Rutgers University undergraduate, O'Keefe videotaped a classmate distributing to a Women in Culture and Society lecture a handout that emphasized that a "good wife always knows her place."

And most tastefully of all, O'Keefe drove around posing as a Publisher's Clearing House van offering big checks to people, only to taunt them that the money is what was going to bank bailouts. Black people sure are suckers for that one!

Do not-so-subtly racist or sexist stunts count as courts of law? Shouldn't there be a requirement that they at least be funny, besides mean for the sake of mean?

Is this same adolescent accountability accepted by defense contractors, when Blackwater and its owner Erik Prince are implicated in murder? He just keeps getting contracts. Rep. Darrel Issa from San Diego sent out a letter bragging of cutting ACORN's money for all of us, then asked us to give him money. San Diego has had political scandals that have led to actual convictions, not simply recordings of speculative conversations. Isn't it time to slash San Diego's federal funding? All of this is not to get off subject, though. Whatever angry conservatives want to insist the subject is.

It is natural for many to shirk away from defending ACORN in light of this footage. But this particular exchange is not just cherry-picked — it was planted, nurtured, and harvested, the latest to take down an organization that empowers the numbers that vote Republicans out of office.

CHAPTER 36

The Lynching of ACORN

11/30/2009

In his confirmation hearings for the Supreme Court, Clarence Thomas refuted Professor Anita Hill's sexual harassment testimony against him with these famous words:

"This is a case in which this sleaze, this dirt, was searched for by staffers of members of this committee, was then leaked to the media, and this committee and this body validated it and displayed it at prime time over our entire nation....This is a circus. It's a national disgrace. And from my standpoint as a black American, as far as I'm concerned, it is a high-tech lynching for uppity blacks who in any way deign to think for themselves, to do for themselves, to have different ideas, and it is a message that unless you kowtow to an old order, this is what will happen to you. You will be lynched, destroyed, caricatured by a committee of the US Senate rather than hung from a tree."

I cite this as precedent in three realms: An African-American defining a lynching beyond the traditional mob beating and hanging of black people; a Supreme Court Justice not known for opinions sympathetic to minorities here asserting racism as the cause in a line of inquiry; and the U.S. Congress's acceptance of this definition as they hastily approved the minimally experienced Thomas following his scathing complaints.

The history of lynching in America is considerable. From 1882-1968, nearly 5000 lynchings occurred in the United States. Lynching is vigilantism and extrajudicial decision by a group of people, a violent act by a mob that does not believe their agenda will be met by law, aware they are acting out of the law, but in effect being the law. There is rarely accountability for those involved. In fact, the display of the victim hanging for all to see is meant to scare off others, violators of perceived segregation or threats to authority. A perceived wrong to white women was often used as justification. Fueled by prejudice and mistruths, urged by a perceived threat or need for immediate justice, lynchings often occurred for reasons other than the alleged crime, like a land or business dispute. Lynchings occurred primarily with blacks men dying at the hands of a white mob, but white people were also targeted, for activism or outspokenness.

By the standard of a high-tech lynching, ACORN's travails are commensurate. The attacks on ACORN have been ongoing, involving the Justice Department, the White House, and the Republican National Committee, well before a couple of privileged white kids in costumes wandered into poor communities across the country hoping to make social workers look stupid and lose their jobs. This is a mob Karl Rove started years ago.

James O'Keefe III is serving Karl Rove, knowingly or unknowingly. His very identification of ACORN as what had to be taken down a notch — not Goldman Sachs, not the Treasury, not U.S. companies with off-shore accounts — why would O'Keefe even know what ACORN is?

An extensive report on the media's failure to objectively cover ACORN, just released by the Occidental

College Urban & Environmental Policy Institute shows the rampant inequity of media coverage and lack of accuracy in reporting on ACORN for the past year. If someone were to see solely this much negative press, they would probably hold an unfavorable view of ACORN as well, as some 67% people do, according to a recent poll Karl Rove tweeted.

Enter James O'Keefe III to take that ball of misinformation and run with it. On FOX & Friends, James O'Keefe III is introduced at the beginning of the interview, wearing a fur coat over his preppy blazer, as he waves a cane. The host is quick to excuse his appearance: "You're not a pimp, you're just playing one on our show."

O'Keefe replies: "I'm one of the whitest guys ever, I just wear ridiculous stuff and put people in ridiculous situations." That is how he assures us he is not a pimp—he is one of the Whitest Guys Ever, therefore on the opposite end of the spectrum from the Blackest Guys Ever, who normally tend to this kind of thing.

Implicit is this: 'I am so white, I had to dress up like a pimp caricature to look black, and it actually worked. That they acknowledged me despite my outlandish attire shows that they are so gullible and base, I was mistaken for a real pimp, which they all must know, being minorities. Once disguised in this clownish attire, they spoke to me as one of their own, so therefore this is how they all behave throughout their organization. Had I not been dressed as Huggy Bear from Starsky & Hutch, the ACORN employees would have known that I was white, and therefore been on their best behavior, as we can expect them to be to us white people when we come around to check on them.'

Just by walking in the door dressed like this, O'Keefe is casting aspersions that people like this would go there (not just sex workers—clueless sex workers). O'Keefe even pleaded with one alarmed ACORN worker to not call the cops for assistance, so that later O'Keefe can fault him for not calling the cops. As O'Keefe says in the above clip coldly, "That's who these people are."

O'Keefe is quick to generalize an entire national organization based on a singular intrusive experience, despite other ACORN offices not taking his bait, after admitting he went in there to prove they were thugs. If that's who these people really are, why not release the videotapes in their entirety to show that, including those tapes shot in cities that did not humor O'Keefe, like Los Angeles or Philadelphia, where the ACORN office filed a police report about the pimp and ho spectacle?

As O'Keefe insists in the clip above, ACORN's allegation that the tapes appear doctored is "a lie," so he shouldn't have a problem proving it by releasing the full unedited tapes, which would likely be part of ACORN"s lawsuit against him. Refuting the "moral equivalence," O'Keefe decries that doctoring tapes does not even compare with child prostitution — suggesting that to O'Keefe, the ends justify the means. Was this about the truth, or making ACORN look bad?

Lost in all of the sensationalism of O'Keefe's hyperbole and selective truths was that there has been no other connection between ACORN and underage prostitution, until O'Keefe walked in and started talking about it to any ACORN employee he could get to listen to him.

Try to explain this to the anti-ACORN vandalism that appeared immediately after O'Keefe's videos, notably at Shepard Fairy's art studio in Santa Monica. The stencil reading "ACORN Funded Prostitution Zone" doesn't take into account that there has been no evidence of actual prostitution, or that Shepard Fairy doesn't even have any connection to ACORN—but he made a poster for Obama, so they're all connected? This is the kind of hasty reaction that ties a bunch of unrelated things together in a mob's mind, searching for some easy target.

Many in the crankosphere were quick to chest-beat: "To defend ACORN is to defend child prostitution itself. No one can defend them now!" Actually, you can defend ACORN, and many have, because decades of real work in communities across our country still amounts to more than a fleeting image to a bunch of anonymous people in Gotcha Mode who do not know the reality of what ACORN is and will not bother to learn.

But once again, this is beside the point: Do I have to defend everything that ACORN has or has not done to decry this unjust process? Myself and others have attested to ACORN's greater good, but there is a critical need to refute gross misrepresentation and be vigilant in truth to rebuff future pitchfork-wavers.

In the wake of the fallout from the Pimp-Ho videos, the first government tie to drop ACORN was the Census Bureau, even though they do not pay ACORN for their service. Rep. Daniel Issa of Orange County introduced a measure to strip ACORN of all federal funding, which quickly passed with few questions. It passed so quickly, no one realized it could apply to all defense contractors, as it might should. Now, Democrats are falling over each other trying to score a major win for Republicans and enact a new measure to re-de-fund ACORN, just to be safe.

This is another characteristic of lynching: That it is not just the hate mongers doing it. This was carried out by the community. James Allen's Without Sanctuary, a book of postcards from the turn of the 20th century when lynching photos were like trading cards, includes this observation from Pulitzer Prize-winning historian Leon F. Litwack wrote:

"The photographs stretch our credulity, even numb our minds and senses to the full extent of the horror, but they must be examined if we are to understand how normal men and women could live with, participate in, and defend such atrocities, even reinterpret them so they would not see themselves or be perceived as less than civilized. The men and women who tortured, dismembered, and murdered in this fashion understood perfectly well what they were doing and thought of themselves as perfectly normal human beings. Few had any ethical qualms about their actions. This was not the outburst of crazed men or uncontrolled barbarians but the triumph of a belief system that defined one people as less human than another. For the men and women who comprised these mobs, as for those who remained silent and indifferent or who provided scholarly or scientific explanations, this was the highest idealism in the service of their race. One has only to view the self-satisfied expressions on their faces as they posed beneath black people hanging from a rope or next to the charred remains of a Negro who had been burned to death. What is most disturbing about these scenes is the discovery that the perpetrators of the crimes were ordinary people, not so different from ourselves - merchants, farmers, laborers, machine operators, teachers, doctors, lawyers, policemen, students; they were family men and women, good churchgoing folk who came to believe that keeping black people in their place was nothing less than pest control, a way of combating an epidemic or virus that if not checked would be detrimental to the health and security of the community."

James Allen himself reflects on the postcards of lynchings as pornographic fodder:

"I believe the photographer was more than a perceptive spectator at lynchings. The photographic art played as significant a role in the ritual as torture or souvenir grabbing - a sort of two-dimensional biblical swine, a receptacle for a collective sinful self. Lust propelled their commercial reproduction and distribution, facilitating the endless replay of anguish. Even dead, the victims were without sanctuary."

On James O'Keefe III's Facebook page, one of his many new supporters posted, 'Is there some way to outlaw ACORN? And then anyone giving them money would be breaking the law.' While such strong federal government intervention seems to be counter to the Right's constant outcry of preventing such intrusion, it does aspire to bend the law to punish those who disagree, and set an example.

In no way am I suggesting that O'Keefe was, or is, consciously promoting racial violence, or even responsible for any that occurs in the wake of his smear job.

But at a lynching a hundred years ago, James O'Keefe III would have been the one taking the picture.

CHAPTER 37

Leonard Zeskind: A History of White Nationalism

07/26/2010

In a tumultuous month of racial discourse — the pro-slavery sentiments of the Tea Party Express leader, the smearing of Shirley Sherrod, the faux-troversy over "New Black Panthers," the ratcheting of anti-immigrant rancor — a refrain of outrage has become the norm. That this outrage has consistently been coming from white conservatives seems indicative of a crest in a country that has lived under slavery as long as it hasn't.

This white backlash has been metastasizing over decades and has worn many mantles, argues Leonard Zeskind, author of the engrossing book, *Blood and Politics: The History of the White Nationalist Movement from the Margins to the Mainstream*. Zeskind has spent many years following the movements' leaders and attending gatherings, developing a unique insight into the membership, mindsets, and resources comprising a diaspora of Klansmen and Holocaust deniers, anti-immigration forces and militia men, executives in offices and everyday Americans.

Stressing a chasm of cultural difference between Middle America and the Coasts, Zeskind explained to me in this sit-down interview that many of the mainstream mouthpieces bemoaning the disenfranchised white man are hardly influential, but rather pandering to an existent culture ingrained with separatism.

Zeskind places the origin of this self-martyrdom at the repeal of the Jim Crow laws back under the Civil Rights Act in 1964. As alienation under loss of privilege set in, the defense of America's identity as a white nation became a unifying cause. In the years since, spurred by a preeminent entitlement to America, some form of white nationalism has continually emerged, often making headway into the mainstream.

Concurrently, there have been strident efforts by white power vanguardists to isolate and attract their own followers, in a long-term struggle to reclaim the reins of domestic dominance. Zeskind artfully weaves an historical narrative investigating these two camps in the white nationalist movement by following the trails of two leaders that embody opposing philosophies: Willis Carto and William Pierce, who built rivaling political and financial machines.

To ask Zeskind about the presence of the white nationalist voice today, he is obliged to provide an historical context for the part of America that has been innately intolerant—asserting that not only have these forces been years in the building, they are constantly adjusting core ideology to contemporary circumstances to update and expand the cause of white nationalism, demanding our vigilance. I solicited his assessment on an array of influences conflating our modern ethnological tempest.

On the Tea Party

ZESKIND: In the 50s and 60s the Ku Klux Klan and the citizens councils were trying to preserve a Jim Crow society. They were trying to preserve the status quo. In the 70's and 80's they came to realize that that movement that society was gone, and so their stated goals was to overturn the current society. They were no longer defending the status quo, they were trying to oppose the status quo, to turn over the status quo.

Out of that phenomenon came the notion of the white victim. The dispossessed majority—in their own term —the grouping of white people who saw themselves no longer as having the prerogatives and privileges of the ruling group. They saw that this the first move towards multiracial democracy turned white people into victims. This is of course a false notion that any objective analysis of the facts of American life would prove, that white people still have the upper hand on every aspect. Everything from getting a job to getting a house to getting abank loan to passing on their wealth to their children to even until your health and happiness and society. Those things still remain overwhelmingly privileges of white folks.

But these folks had invented the notion of the white victim, the dispossessed majority. The Tea Parties have come to embody that notion of victimhood, albeit in a different way than it was articulated, say, by the Ku Klux Klan in the 70's and 80's, or albeit differently than it was articulated by some of the philosophers of the movement at that time.

But it is nonetheless a movement that feels like they've lost their country and to use their own slogan, they want it back. They feel like they've lost the country, not that they've lost their individual standing, not that they've lost their job, but that they've lost their country and they want their country, their nationhood back. So it's a nationalist movement. It's a nationalist movement that embodies a re-articulated notion of this dispossessed majority white victimhood.

I don't think these things are economically-driven. Now, I think the fact that we have economic problems makes for a fertile territory, but it's not because people are unemployed, because the unemployed people aren't in the tea parties, the unemployed people don't buy massive amounts of guns and pay dues to the National Rifle Association. The unemployed people are barely surviving and they're not part of this.

On the Birthers

ZESKIND: So-called "Birthers" are the people that don't believe President Barack Obama hasa real, live, natural-born American citizenship, he doesn't have his birth certificate to prove it. This focus on "Natural Born citizenship" is interesting in the Barack Obama case for a couple of reasons: one, he ran against John McCain and nobody raised it, although John McCain had been actually born in Panama in the Panama Canal Zone, and nobody said boo about that.

It's Barack Obama's skin color that excites the birthers, if you will, and causes them to discount his own, real-life, natural-born American-ness. Because he must be an alien, he's got an alien name, he went to countries where Islam was a majority, so he must be an alien, and therefore he could not be a natural-born American in this world view. That's what's important about it.

What else is important about it is, it's attached in a policy wonk kind of way to the fight over the 14th amendment. The 14th amendment is the amendment to the Constitution passed after the Civil War that guarantees people equal treatment before the law, and it's the thing that brought citizenship to the former slaves. And so it says in the 14th amendment, if you are born in the United States then you are a citizen of the United States, even if your grandparents parents and all your aunts and uncles were illegal or undocumented aliens, if you were born in the United States, you're a natural-born citizen. And so the Birthers are very much of the ilk that says, "No, there's a certain type of person that's of natural-born American and all you others, we really don't want you." And so you see a lot of tie up between the so-called Birthers and the anti-immigrant nativist types, both in the house and the Senate and in the social movements.

On Anti-Immigration Laws

ZESKIND: There's been various successive stages about the immigrant and the immigrant activity. I want to stress to you that the issue in immigration is skin color and Spanish-speaking -ness. If these were all, you know, Canadians who cross the border and were members of the Presbyterian Church, we wouldn't hear about it.

And so the skin color and Spanish speaking are the salient issues in this movement. And what happened is, they tried to stop immigration reform in the spring of 2006, they succeeded at it. They knew that their movement was stronger than the immigrant rights movement, which has remained true to this day. The anti-immigrant folks then decided that since they couldn't get enforcement policies passed at federal government, that they'd adopted an attrition strategy, a strategy of making life miserable for the immigrants.

And so what you see in Arizona is an outgrowth of that turn away from federal policy and towards more directly making life miserable for the immigrants. And so what you see in Arizona is an attempt to make life miserable for people. They're not done, but they're winning that battle, the anti-immigrant people, they're winning that battle. they are forcing people to move, they are making life miserable for people, and the immigrants rights community needs to figure out a response that looks ahead to the next battle rather than fighting the last battle.

On Palin, Beck, Limbaugh, & Breitbart

ZESKIND: Well, Sarah Palin's claim to fame with the Tea Parties is her invocation of "Real Americans" versus, I don't know what, fake Americans? Americans who weren't real? Sarah Palin, that was her contribution to this conversation. But it must be said that when she spoke at a Tea Party Nation convention and received a $100,000 speaking fee, a lot of the other Tea Parties walked out of that convention because they didn't want to help pay her fee.

So she's not really a spokesperson for the Tea Parties per se, but people think of her that way, so she's adopted some of those attributes of the Tea Parties. But if she were to become the Republican presidential candidate, God forbid, you'd see a lot of the Tea Party types clashing with

Sarah Palin because they know that she's a spokesperson but she's also a showboat interested only in herself.

There is a difference—and I think that people have to grasp this—there's a difference in politics, culture-defining ideas, between the coasts and the middle West and the South part of the country, the so-called Heartland. There are differences in approach and style of life and everything, and frankly we're just not as liberal in the middle of the country as we are on the coasts. So things that matter on the coast do not matter as much in the interior of the country.

It's not Glenn Beck so much as that audience that matters. If Glenn Beck didn't have an audience and all he did was yammer all the time on the radio and nobody listened to him, we wouldn't be talking about him. Who is his audience? It's these middle Americans that are trying to protect their privileges and think that they've been dispossessed. Glenn Beck speaks to them. Glenn Beck has been become, more than Sarah Palin, actually, a spokesperson for those Americans who think of themselves in that way.

But there's also people who operate independently of all that and who don't depend on the Glenn Beck's of the world, don't think Sarah Palin is so whoopee, and are very much part of the Tea Party movement, and very much part of the ancillary movements around the Tea Parties—the Oath Keepers, the various militias that's been off, and so forth. They don't need Sarah Palin to tell them what to think. They don't need Glenn Beck to tell them what to think. Glenn Beck ratifies what they already think. Glenn Beck gets his ideas from them. But it's their social movement that has created the Glenn Beck's, and not the reverse.

Rush Limbaugh is, you know, a buffoon and a clown and we all see him as a buffoon and a clown. Some great books were written where they sort of took him apart. I think a lot of people listen to Rush Limbaugh just because it's afternoon radio at work and they're on the shop floor, and there's a jackass up there making a fool of himself and so they listen to him. I think the Republican Party pays attention to him, or at least some people in the Republican Party pay attention to him. But I don't know that he has a power to shape these things, I would say the same thing about him that I would say about Glenn Beck: he wouldn't exist if the constituency wasn't there.

Andrew Breitbart has been a dirty tricks operator. The fact that he's part of the Tea Party movement, or that he speaks at Tea Party events now is a result of the fact that the Tea Party emerged, he didn't help the Tea Parties emerge. But once the Tea Parties emerged he saw a milieu in which his dirty tricks made sense. But that's really what he's about, he is of the old school. If he had been a Nixon plumber, you know, we would have recognized it. He's not a Nixon plumber, but he is a dirty tricks operator.

I don't know for certain that Andrew Breitbart wants to take down every black person, but it appears that every person that he tries to take down is black. Because this group of Tea Partiers and conservative radicals, etc., do not like black people to have the same rights as white people, it's more or less that simple. There's no rights that these white people want to respect. And they don't like to have to. And they may say it's about ideology, and they may say it's about

Left, and they may say it's about Right, but it's not. It's that they're trying to bring down people of color.

The Future

ZESKIND: We're the most powerful country in the world and if we become more democratic minded, if we become less warlike, if we become more racially just, we will have benefited every country in the world. And that's a good way to look at it, as far as I'm concerned. In 32 years —if you were to have a child today, it would be 32 years old —white people become a demographic minority in a nation of minorities. We will have to learn to get along. We will have to not only learn how to get along, we're gonna have to learn how to share amongst ourselves. Let's share power, share politics, and share the bounty of this good, good country. The sweat of everybody's labor, it's going to have to be part of the common good. It can't be held out for the private white prerequisite. You won't be able to do it. We better get prepared for that, now. The Tea Partiers are getting prepared. They're trying to make sure that when that time comes white people have all the power back. 'Take our country back.' We have to be prepared for the battle to come over racial justice in this country.

CHAPTER 38

It's Not Sarah Palin's Fault

01/10/2011

It's not Sarah Palin's fault that some guy went and shot some people in Tucson, any more than it's *Taxi Driver*'s fault that some guy went and shot Ronald Reagan to impress Jodie Foster. For one, there are no accounts whatsoever of Sarah Palin's whereabouts being in the vicinity of the shooting (even though her daughter Bristol did just move into her new Arizona home less than two hours away).

The responsibility of a gunman ultimately lies in their deciding to become what will invariably be described as a "gunman" — being the one operating a gun. Jared Lee Loughner is widely reported to be the shooter taken into custody, but it was also widely reported that Rep. Gabrielle Giffords was dead, until it was reported that she was in surgery and then looked likely to survive. Pima County Sheriff Clarence Dupnik blamed the attack on the violent rhetoric that has become the voice of accepted right wing discourse:

"When you look at unbalanced people, how they respond to the vitriol that comes out of certain mouths about tearing down the government. The anger, the hatred, the bigotry that goes on in this country is getting to be outrageous," he said. "And unfortunately, Arizona, I think, has become the capital. We have become the mecca for prejudice and bigotry."

A perusal of Jared Lee Loughner's YouTube videos give a convincing first impression of crazy. Having edited graphics, text, and music a lot over the years, just a few seconds of looking at his nonsensical messages in small, off-centered type with weird electronic music convinced me, professionally speaking, that this guy was complete crazy pants. The pathetic burning of an American flag in the woods while wearing trash bags? These little videos are disconcerting and creepy like that haunting VHS tape in The Ring tried to be, but instead ended up looking like a music video by Nine Inch Nails.

It's not like if Fox News were a little less incendiary, this guy wouldn't be having violent fantasies. In what constitutes a massacre, as well as a brazen act of domestic terrorism, there will no doubt be endless review of the killer's background and lead-up to this tragic day of shooting 18 people, killing six, including a 9-year-old girl. All the warning signs are always there in hindsight.

But this isn't Sarah's fault.

As soon as the shooting occurred, the Internet lit up with people pointing out that Sarah Palin had put a gun sight target over Giffords' district as a target, which was controversial at the time for being incendiary. Sarah even kept it up after election day when she Tweeted:

"Remember months ago, a "bullseye" icon used 2 target the 20 Obamacare-lovin' incumbent seats? We won 18 out of 20 (90% success rate; T'aint bad)"

But now, to Sarah, all this linking of her gun talk to gun rampages is just the Gotcha Media at it again.

To Sarah, she is as blameless for the guy shooting an elected government official that she happened to target as Paul Schaeder, Martin Scorsese, and Robert DeNiro are not responsible for John Hinckley shooting Ronald Reagan after seeing Taxi Driver. To Sarah, it's all just a manufactured image of violence that everybody tries on and people like it. Even though it was Rep. Gabrielle Giffords herself who warned after being targeted in Palin's crosshairs:

I mean, this is a situation where — I mean, people don't — they really need to realize that the rhetoric and firing people up and, you know, even things, for example, we're on Sarah Palin's targeted list. But the thing is that the way that she has it depicted has the crosshairs of a gunsight over our district. When people do that, they've gotta realize there's consequences to that action.

To Sarah, it's easy to stake out that tough talk invoking guns, targets, bulls-eyes, etc., because no one else is using it (probably because they knew it could sound bad). But after bragging of her hunting background, it's been revealed on her own reality show that she does not even know much about guns or how to use them.

She's not in politics for the sake of guns. It's about her. It's about being contrarian to whatever got said by the person she wants to be. If Michele Obama wants to fight the epidemic of childhood obesity, Sarah Palin feigns outrage that Michele is trying to take away your right to dessert. Even the Wall Street Journal dryly surmised last month, "Mrs. Palin would be more effective if she made some distinctions among the Obama policies that really are worth opposing."

And as long as she gets recognition for it, good or bad, there is no distinction to her, just like in her perverted sense of celebrity culture, the logical road to the White House is through Reality TV. If it's about her, she's winning.

But today, for once, I suspect she might not like the attention she's getting. Sure, her words have come back to haunt her before when she took positions just to get a crowd chanting mantras like "Drill, Baby, Drill!" But it took her a week to respond to the Deepwater Horizon explosion and the BP/Halliburton/TransOcean disaster, in a Tweet. After the shooting in Tucson, Palin's site quickly scrubbed that picture of targets on congress, and she offered "sincere condolences" in a hasty, detached statement that read like a memo about war casualties. Not so much on her favorite catchphrase today, "Don't retreat — reload!"

Blaming Sarah Palin for the outbreaks of violence that happen by nuts who even remotely engage in her arbitrary incitements is, to a degree, like pinning violence on Quentin Tarantino because of his sensationalism of violence. Quentin Tarantino may have inspired some derivative movies, (including his own) but despite his unrealistic pornographic obsession, it's unlikely he has ever experienced real violence firsthand, and less likely to be the sole motivator for some other nut to suddenly decide to get violent.

Same with Sarah Palin. Why should there be any consequence to anything she should have to say or do? Since when do any American politicians accept responsibility for anything of their own, or actually face law enforcement? She shouldn't even have to finish her job as governor, because people were attacking her by asking questions about her job as governor, when she could make money talking about herself instead.

When there are negative facts in print about her, as throughout her campaigning on repeated lies and distortions for McCain, she blames the liberal press because they hate her, but not for reasons that should matter like what she says or does, but for other reasons, like because they're jealous, which is what her daughters seem to have learned to accuse their detractors of.

But the reality is, Sarah Palin gets an inordinate amount of media coverage because she outrages more people than she inspires. Networks: they really do not care why you are watching. Blogs? Are you kidding? They count clicks in one way, and anything Palin-related gets clicks. What is lost on the news sources is that part of the backlash against her is because of her ongoing media coverage despite any real news-making. People can't believe that other people take her seriously, and people do, because she's always in the news, which traditionally connotes "relevance," "importance," "stature," "influence," "impact," "a thing that matters."

Our news media blogosphere culture lost sight at some point and accepted a Republican ploy from an elderly presidential ticket as the new reliable royal to love and/or hate. The media has unfurled her catty divisive comments as though they were a pertinent development from a head of state. The media doesn't care, either, they just want your validation by getting out your hatred through their day's work.

We need adults to tell hysterical children to calm down and behave and stop acting like spoiled selfish brats, because you are embarrassing everybody right now. This means the media calling out hate speech for what it is, identifying terrorism for what it is, and not creating a self-sustaining empty spokesperson of blame by reporting on anything Sarah Palin says. If the media limited itself to covering what Sarah Palin does rather than says, it'd be limited to printing press releases about her appearances on reality shows.

Right now, to Sarah Palin, she herself is the victim in this situation. It's not that she wants people to go shoot her political enemies; for one, it looks really bad, obviously. She wants people to be incited enough with vitriol to listen to her and do what she says, but not alienate the mainstream she desperately wants to be accepted by.

When you are projecting victimhood constantly on your followers, however, it is possible that some people are already so alienated, this manufactured force of celebrity media, political vanity, and fear mongering sends these troubled individuals over the edge.

It's not Sarah Palin and her rhetoric that make crazy people do crazy things. It's making her crazy rhetoric matter that does.

CHAPTER 39

Rupert Murdoch Shows the Need for Oversight

07/20/2011

In their testimony before the House of Commons yesterday, Rupert and James Murdoch insisted on their ignorance about the phone hacking and bribery scandal that engulfed their publication News of the World and led to the resignation of top editors and police officials.

In their shaky recriminations against the people who worked for their people, it's a wonder the Murdochs would know much of anything that goes on in their newspapers. For NOTW editor and Murdoch confidante Rebekah Brooks to not know the genesis of thousands of stories she was in meetings deciding upon defies plausibility. For NOTW staff members to organize a conspiracy to pay off cops for leads and hack into over 4,000 voicemails — without their supervising editor knowing where so much money was coming from and to — those are some very proactive, amazingly clandestine tabloid journalists breaking a myriad of laws at great personal risk.

If Rupert Murdoch is to be believed, as he would desperately like to be, then his loyal staff let him down by not doing the right thing, and coming to tell him about the massive hacking and bribery thingy that they happened to find out about and also knew was wrong. If he is not to be believed, the conclusion to be drawn is the same nonetheless: real government oversight is needed because so many laws are being broken, the idea of "corporate responsibility" is an oxymoron.

It's not just a bribery scandal Scotland Yard spent years trying to keep quiet, nor is it solely the privacy invasions of crime victims. Whistleblowers who first led to this story breaking are starting to die. Between discredited police and intimidated journalists, who knows if these highly suspicious deaths will be deemed foul play. But in everything from media consolidation to electronic privacy to public corruption and informant protection, it's tragically apparent that people don't police themselves well, and that includes the police.

Much of this scandal surrounding the Murdoch empire pertains to keeping the tabloid mill churning — hacking voicemails to get scoops to sell more papers making more money to pay off cops to help you get more scoops. NOTW was the top tabloid paper in Britain until ending its 186 years in fiery disgrace. Similar revelations may yet emerge, from other tabloids in Britain or from other Murdoch media companies.

Where the salacious culture of Royal gossip and Spice Girl updates have made tabloids a defining aspect of England's classist society, Murdoch's media aspirations were targeted at Americans to appeal to their basest cultural cravings: sanctity for nostalgia posing as patriotism, self-important indignation, and fear of others (like those injuns).

Seeing the act of Mr. Burns and Smithers before members of Parliament made me recognize that however divisive and misleading FOX News is, it was just another money-making gambit featuring hot models. Roger Ailes turned FOX News into the partisan dragon that it is today. Rupert Murdoch doesn't actually seem particularly beholden to lawmakers, probably because he believes he makes the laws. Bush speechwriter David Frum said last year, "The Republicans originally thought that Fox works for us, and now we're discovering we work for Fox."

In recognizing how FOX News pushes outrage in all forms at all time, it might be an opportunity now for Republican leaders to take this time to free themselves from the petulance of FOX's xenophobic mantras, and realize that they are bigger slaves to their news cycle than anyone. Because government oversight — looking out for its citizens best interest — cannot happen when government leaders are working night and day to impress a cable news producer, who may as well be a reality TV producer restless for drama.

Government oversight goes even further than not being a publicity whore. The newly formed Consumer Financial Protection Bureau could be an opportunity to re-imagine how the government works to protect its citizens. Yet even though Obama opted to not nominate Elizabeth Warren to a surely partisan battle, and instead tapped former Ohio AG Richard Cordray, Republicans are expected to fight the appointment nonetheless. Republicans seem to fight any attempt at oversight, and it probably has to do with all the money they get from businesses that they are trying to deregulate.

But in what name is this constant cry for deregulation? What do business leaders implore the White House over and over to stave off paying a little more? 'It's bad for business. What hurts me hurts you. Make me pay more and

I will threaten your economy — not to make threats. But, to make threats, we'll spend a lot of money we just said we couldn't afford on ads against you.'

Well, here's what we've learned so far, Cassandras of Capitalism: If you cut taxes for the rich for ten years, they don't spend it on creating jobs, they spend it on politicians to cut their taxes lower. You can change the laws to allow for one media mogul to own multiple newspapers, radio, and TV stations in a single market, but that mogul doesn't have to be accountable as the owner when those media outlets break laws.

It's the cliché conservative Catch-22 of refusing responsibility for others then acting astonished when others loot the treasury; or vilifying government intrusion while counting on corporate tax breaks (i.e., "welfare queens"); or redefining commodities trading to where the high-priced commodity in question doesn't technically really exist as such.

Rupert Murdoch obviously needs help overseeing his vast media empire: NewsCorp needs to be investigated by the Federal Bureau of Investigation, the Federal Communications Commission, and the Federal Elections Commission.

PART SIX

Occupy Wall Street

CHAPTER 40

The Endgame of Occupy Wall Street is Critical Mass

10/06/2011

What is surprisingly unique about the Occupy Wall Street demonstration, and supporting actions across the country, is the broad immediate support without an immediately stated objective. With so little coverage and a yet unspecified goal, major unions lent their support, supportive occupations cropped up nationwide, and the numbers in Liberty Park are growing despite NYPD crackdowns.

Unlike anti-war marches, Tea Party gatherings, or other well-worn modes of protest, the notion of an in-person response to Wall Street's unchecked looting of the economy apparently did not need much explaining. That is because many Americans have been living with painful awareness that their hardships in recent years are related in a myriad of ways to reckless trading, predatory loans, and manifold illegal banking practices, all perpetrated by the same executives still receiving multi-million dollar bonuses whose guilt is trumped by the notion that their companies are Too Big To Fail.

None of these many abuses by financial institutions collectively referred to as Wall Street are new information. It's not like people just flooded the streets upon hearing that Bank of America is trying to tack on another surcharge, just after laying off over 30,000 employees, just after widespread manipulation of their loan business was deemed not criminal, by their own accord. (No, that move by B of A was just easy pickings for Democrats trying to remember their purpose.)

It's not like Americans did not wait while the federal government negotiated good-faith interest-free loans to keep huge banks and firms afloat, at the price to taxpayers, many of whom were struggling to stay afloat themselves under variable interest or inflated mortgages foisted upon them by said financial giants. It's not like financial regulations weren't proposed to Congress, with larger reforms left by the wayside, and in the final decision by the Federal Reserve on the Durbin Amendment of the Dodd-Frank Financial Act, credit card companies somehow get to charge more for debit swipes than they had even hoped. Bank lobbyists paid off, in more than one sense.

And, it's not like President Obama hasn't trotted out some fine rhetoric of late, angling the ongoing Republican obstructionism to fuel his re-election campaign as it gears up. Yes, it's math, not class warfare. But, if this were a metaphor of head to head competition between classes — namely, the top 1% Super Rich that owns 40% of the wealth versus the 99% rest of Americans — then Obama would be like a goalie, constantly swarmed by the offensive John Boehner, Mitch McConnell, Eric Cantor, Darrell Issa, bank lobbyists, and Goldman Sachs alumni in his own ranks. The Super Rich Team will continue to score point after point on Obama, because despite his considerable skill set, it's like he's playing at the company picnic, and really, you just don't make your bosses look bad when they underwrite your existence.

Obama is looking for $1 billion to fund his re-election campaign. That may seem extraordinary, but after the disastrous Supreme Court decision Citizens United vs. FEC, it is a given that there will be even more spent against him in anonymous corporate money. Karl Rove's American Crossroads and Crossroads GPS have announced plans to raise and spend record amounts, over $300 million in outside ads running across the country in the 2012 races.

Obama is not going to get one billion dollars from $5 donations, no matter how many email blasts. Obama and his team have been currying favor like a schoolboy with Wall Street throughout this administration because they are waiting for the pay-off in their campaign coffers. The slap on the wrist following the financial meltdown was more drying their hands like a bathroom attendant so they can get back to work making important deals without consequence.

While the financial meltdown and ensuing bailouts came before Obama, the lack of reform or accountability does not win him any gratitude from either side, it only serves as precedent that selling bundled crap mortgages to old people goes unpunished. In fact, it is richly rewarded. Obama's deference and endless capital to the banking industry has long made it clear where his priorities are. His jobs plan is well-intentioned, but probably a drop in the bucket and a few years late. For all the bitter clamor over health care reform, it's quite likely that it will be deemed impermissible by the Supreme Court. Clarence Thomas can't wait to sit silently through the arguments before he punts our healthcare system back to the wolves that employ his wife, Ginni.

As the crowds grow, this will become Obama's next oil spill. How long will he let Occupy Wall Street go on before addressing it as more than just a policy point to support his agenda? Many loyalists will defend the intentions and constraints on Obama, but this much is painfully clear: The President must act now. Because if he does not get in front of this parade, it's about to surpass him.

If Obama really does aspire to be like President Lincoln, then he must recognize that his country is rent apart and it requires a true leader to keep our union from collapsing under debt and looted public services.

Because when people show up at the gates of their oppressor, the response is not: "What do you want? Can you bullet-point it for me?" You know what this is about. Our country has been decimated over the past three years, with continual revelations of financial impropriety, concerted fraud, and executive compensation the amount of a small nation's GDP. This might be the one protest where, if asked why you were there, you could reply, "Are you fucking kidding me?" and that would actually be understood.

To dispel media misconceptions, here's what Occupy Wall Street is not: it's not another Tea Party, a corporate PAC-backed stab at populism consisting of right wing extremists. It's not just young people in attendance, even though younger generations have more to lose anyway, and many are already crippled with student debt and no job possibilities. (Admittedly, younger people are better suited to sleep in inconvenient places and be fine with that. The kids call this "crashing," which should not be interpreted as a roughhousing sort of thing.)

Occupy Wall Street is not anti-capitalism. We don't live in capitalism. Capitalism is supposed to be merit based and left to the market — consumers — to decide where innovation and service is found. What has been foisted on us again and again is not a fair and open market. Massive companies spend huge sums to avoid paying taxes altogether. They then spend money to back politicians that will be friendly to them, in terms of regulations and tax breaks or pressure on rivals. This is a system of massive corporate welfare, where the biggest corporations pay the least to the country that allows them to prosper, while they spend their excess money in hopes of making more money through lower taxes, government jobs, or loosened environmental restrictions. Election cycles ensure ongoing opportunities for candidates to be wooed with money or threatened with ads. The more they spend on the race, the more indebted candidates become to their backers. Those that become elected repay their backers with loose oversight, no-bid contracts, and even accept their donors' legislation pre-written. We don't live in capitalism — that's favoritism.

And most importantly, Occupy Wall Street is not one political party or part of a spectrum. This grassroots movement is fundamentally removed from both parties, because both parties accept vast fortunes from Wall Street to not rain on their parade. The reason abuses have thrived is because of the cost of running for office. Most people's political persuasion or identity is based on their own sense of what's just and fair. The nuance of foreign policy or civil liberties is lost when people are losing their homes due to manipulative mortgages from banks that have faced no discipline or reform and have been given federal money to loan to people which they still sit on.

Yet, it will take a political solution to retake our country from the Gollum of Wall Street. There's no way any of these banks or brokers will willingly accept reform measures, even after taking trillions of taxpayer money following their own colossal fuck-ups. Wall Street execs thrive on extracting more and more profit per sale, and get off on boardroom backstabbing. Do you expect them to respond to people of all types camped outside their offices politely? The only thing they care about is if the market goes down.

Real financial overhaul will only happen if we reclaim our elections. We need real campaign reform, and we need to elect the people who will enact it. We do that through running and winning in primaries, where the party's pick usually prevails with the most money. We innovate low budget campaign strategies to support candidates not backed by Political Action Committees, fronts for corporate money. We do it through becoming the media and covering these candidates where we live and across the country. And it starts in the streets. Where else is there but the streets?

America was born in the streets. Our first president was sworn in on the steps of Wall Street, where Congress convened for years. The framer's dream of escaping monarchy is being eclipsed by the wealthiest 1% and their insatiable assault on anything the government provides to the public.

How can we not occupy Wall Street? Wall Street occupies US.

CHAPTER 45

Occupy Our Homes: "I'm Not Leaving"

12/07/2011

December 6, 2011, was a national day of action targeting homes facing foreclosure, organized by a coalition of community groups behind the movement Occupy Our Homes. Protests were held across the country, in cities such as New York, Chicago, Philadelphia, Atlanta, San Francisco, Minneapolis, Portland, OR, and more.

Actions included "reclaiming" houses that banks are leaving vacant, and "home defense" to stop banks from foreclosing and accept payments from the homeowners, which banks like Chase and Wells Fargo are refusing to do in some cases.

Some of the groups involved in the community resistance effort include ACCE (Alliance of Californians for Community Empowerment), The New Bottom Line, Refund California, New York Communities for Change, Occupy Wall Street, Take Back the Land, SOUL (Chicago), SEIU, and The Coffee Party.

In South Gate, CA, twenty minutes south of Los Angeles, dozens of supporters rallied around the home of Ana Casas Wilson, with several pledging to camp out in her front yard while she defies eviction, and face arrest if necessary.

Ana shared her story with the assembled media and demonstrators: living with cerebral palsy and battling stage four breast cancer, she was stalked by loan reps assuring her they could lower her payments for the home she has lived in with her family since 1975. After relenting to get more money for her health care and refinancing in 2005, Ana eventually found that her loan was acquired by Wells Fargo, who has since refused to make any modifications or accept make-up payments.

Ana told the crowd, "Believe me, I would have gotten out of the sick bed and I would've been there when they foreclosed on my house. 'Cause I am not leaving. You don't just get a house every day, and sometimes you don't even get a second chance to get a house. We've been here a long time, we're like fixtures in this city, at least I am. Everybody knows. You know, 'everybody knows your name'? Well everybody knows my name and my face. I've done things in this city that no other disabled person has ever done. So I am not leaving. And somebody asked me, 'What's going to happen if you have to go to jail?' Oh well, I'll just go to jail. At least I know I'll have a roof over my head still."

ACCE leader Lynn Motley announced, "Here we have an example of one of thousands of families who can afford to make payments, but their bank, Wells Fargo, has refused to work with them." She then asked the crowd to take out their phones and call the CEO of Wells Fargo, John Stumpf, to ask that he stop the eviction of Ana Casas Wilson and her family, and work to modify their loan, since they have three steady incomes in their house. An activist and advocate for other disabled Angelenos, Ana has held off the eviction order from being enforced for the time being. Now, she is not alone.

The Occupy Our Homes actions came on the same day that the Attorney Generals of California and Nevada announced a joint investigation into bank practices that precipitated the housing crisis as well as the handling of foreclosures.

Kwazi Nkrumah of Occupy the Hood addressed the crowd: "This is absolutely ridiculous. The banks have taken so many homes they can't even log how many. They're three years behind. It's going to take them three to three and a half years to even account for all the homes they've foreclosed on. This is insane. We have houses standing empty and deteriorating in neighborhoods all over L.A. And simply the deterioration of those homes brings down the property value of every other home near those homes. And so this becomes a game which is about controlling the housing market, and buying cheap and selling dear. The banks are accumulating these homes waiting for a turnaround in the economy where they can jack the prices up again and rip off the same people who they took homes from yesterday. The reality is, we have so many people who are confronting foreclosure on these banks, it is a local disaster hitting our community silently, because they're haven't been enough people speaking out about it. But that's coming to an end."

Pastor Rob Robbins of the SEIU United Long Term Care Workers led the demonstrators in a somber prayer: " "As we are standing here today praying to a perfect God, we ask you Lord to look on this family and the thousands of millions of others who are just a number to the big corporations. But You said, "All souls are mine." You know the hairs on our head, so we ask you today, intercede for the Casa family. Working people everywhere who don't know

221

the sophistication of the high rise and the corporate structure, but we know God."

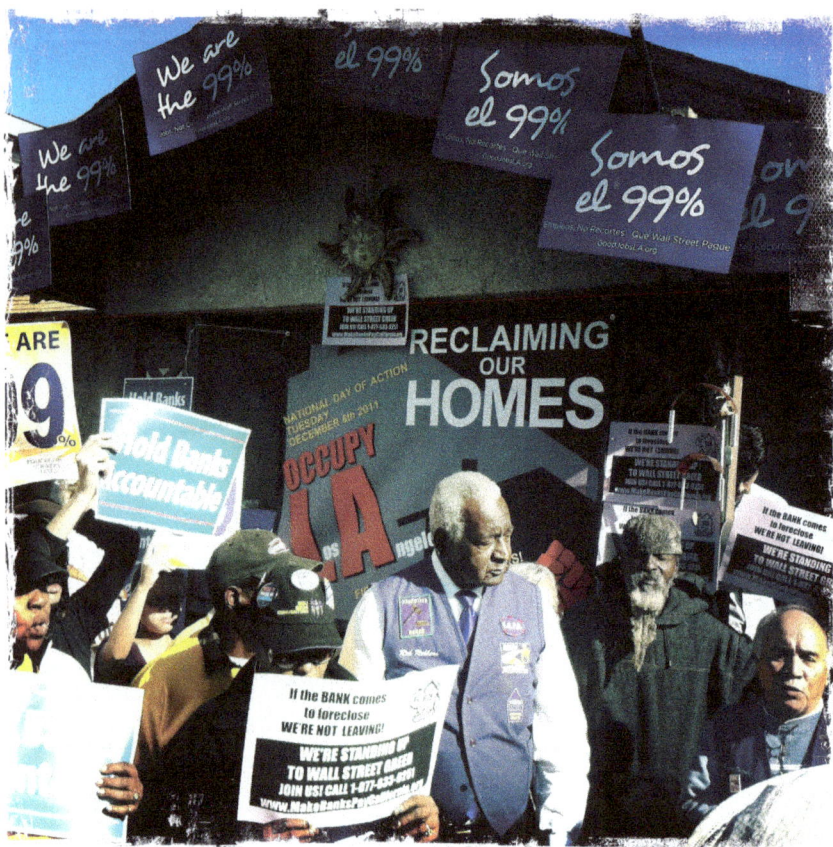

The home of Ana Casas Wilson. Photo by John Wellington Ennis.

CHAPTER 46

Anthem of 2011: "The Show Goes On" by Lupe Fiasco

12/27/2011

2011 has been a pivotal, inspiring year, and a turning point promising big things for 2012. And it's maybe because people were broke and taking to the streets that, culturally, 2011 was somewhat uneventful. I suspect 2012 will bring the creative explosion of a culture reignited by shared awareness and new-found confidence. But looking back at 2011, the seeds of a cultural revolution did not seem to be penetrating the airwaves.

But where most of Hip Hop seemed to descend into a clatter of techno-fused beats and hooks about either partying in the club or partying in the strip club, there stood out a surprisingly positive groove that seems to best put a face on this year of the Occupy genesis.

Weaving an interpolation of Modest Mouse's 2004 upbeat hit "Float On," Lupe Fiasco uses his verses to unify the impoverished and privileged alike, urging courage to resist everyday oppressors, drawing strength from both childhood dreams and the power that a rarefied performer gets to observe when audiences are chanting his lyrics back to him around the world.

And yet in his open-ended challenge that "Ain't nobody leavin, nobody going home, even if they turn the lights on, the show is going on," there seems to be the prescient call for in-person assembly and energy that so many apparently desired deep down, across America, and around the world.

For those who still don't get what the Occupy Wall Street movement has been about, think about it like this: it's a like a vigil for a plan, or an intervention on behalf of an country all too obligingly suffering the painful cuts and deep gouging of corporate greed run amok in our political process. That outrage and alienation turns into empowerment with shared goals and the recognition that the voices of many are suddenly much louder than the voice telling us what additional austerity we should all endure because of some bankers' rampant criminal enterprise, which goes unpunished.

When future generations look back at us and our time, I hope they can associate this song with this tumultuous, inspiring era.

Here are the lyrics and music video for "The Show Goes On" by Lupe Fiasco, from his album *LASERS*.

CHORUS

Alright already the show goes on
All night til the morning we dream so long
Anybody ever wonder when they will see the sun up
Just remember when you come up the show goes on
Alright already the show goes on
All night til the morning we dream so long
Anybody ever wonder when they will see the sun up
Just remember when you come up the show goes on

VERSE 1

Have you ever had the feeling that you was being had
Know that shit that make you mad
They treat you like a slave

Put chains all on your soul
And put whips up on your back
They be lying through they teeth
Hope you slip up off your path
I don't switch up off I just laugh
Put my kicks up on they desk
Unaffected by they threats
Then get busy on they ass
See that's how that chi town made me
That's how my daddy raised me
That glitterin' may not be gold
Don't let nobody play me
If you are my homeboy
You never have to pay me
Gon' and put your hands up
When times is hard you stand up
LUPE the man
Cause a brand that the fans trust
So even if they ban us
They'll never slow my plans up
Chorus
Alright already the show goes on
All night til the morning we dream so long
Anybody ever wonder when they will see the sun up
Just remember when you come up the show goes on
Alright already the show goes on
All night til the morning we dream so long
Anybody ever wonder when they will see the sun up
Just remember when you come up the show goes on

VERSE 2

One in the air for people ain't here
Two in the air for the father that's there
Three in the air for the kids in the ghetto
Four for the kids that don't wanna be there

None for the n——-s tryna hold them back
Five in the air for the teacher not scared
To tell those kids that's living in the ghetto
That the n——-s holding back
That the world is theirs
Yea yea the world is yours
I was once that little boy
Terrified of the world
Now I'm on a world tour
I will give up everything
Even start a world war
For these ghetto girls and boys, I'm rappin' round the world for
Africa to New York
Haiti then I detour
Oakland down to Auckland
Gaza Strip to Detroit
Say hip hop on a destroy
Tell him look at me boy
I hope your son don't have a gun, and never be a D-Boy
Chorus
Alright already the show goes on
All night til the morning we dream so long
Anybody ever wonder when they will see the sun up
Just remember when you come up the show goes on
Alright already the show goes on
All night til the morning we dream so long
Anybody ever wonder when they will see the sun up
Just remember when you come up the show goes on

VERSE 3

So no matter what you been through
No matter what you into
No matter what you see when you look outside your window
Brown grass or green grass
Picket fence or barbed wire

226

Never ever put them down
You just lift your arms higher
Raise them til your arms tired, let em know your there.
That you struggling, surviving that you gon' persevere yea
Ain't nobody leavin', nobody going home
Even if they turn the lights out, the show is going on

CHAPTER 47

Lawrence Lessig: "We've Lost That Republic"

12/29/2011

In this pivotal year of public uproar over the consequences of money in politics, Harvard Professor Lawrence Lessig has attracted considerably more attention to his work in devising a constitutional road map for reform. Yes, that was the former Supreme Court clerk and Stanford copyright expert rousing *The Daily Show*'s studio audience, whose followers Jon Stewart suggested be dubbed "Batmen." His Twitter followers seemed to suddenly jump from several thousand to over 168,000.

With good reason. Of late, there has been a productive discourse articulating the sources of corrupting money in politics and visualizing how our democratic model should work. But the intransigence of those empowered to any meaningful reform is the real problem, and it is in his new book Republic, Lost that Lessig outlines the larger workarounds to our pay-to-play system.

In this interview, Professor Lessig discusses the central problems in approaching a Congress that got there by a system they are reliant on. For one, the identification of the top 1% is off the mark considerably — maxed out campaign contributors account for .05% of the population.

In our culture of expectations for re-election contributions, what develops is a form of extortion, Lessig explains, that has become systematic. What's more, the offices of Congressional workers are so personally influenced by the promise of working for K Street for huge salaries, those staffers are working to please those employers, despite the dismal public opinion of Congress, still at an all time low.

Republic, Lost offers the blueprint many are searching for, with chapter titles such as "How So Damn Much Money Defeats the Left," and "How So Damn Much Money Defeats the Right." Lessig further evokes the highest ideals of the founders in his appeal that despite some core ideological differences with those on the Right, there is widespread support for getting the corruptive influence of corporate money out of the decision-making process of our government. If abolitionists and slave owners could set aside their fundamental differences to author the U.S. Constitution today, and succeed as a nation despite the odds, then that lesson is one we can continue to learn from.

Not About the One Percent

Lessig: If you ever have lived inside of political campaigns or inside of Congress, you recognize the people who have the most influence, the most significant people inside the system are people who max out in their political contributions. So if you ask how many people have maxed out in 2010, 0.05% [point zero five percent] of Americans maxed out in their political contributions. So that means 0.05% have the most influence, and 99.95% don't.

You know Occupy Wall Street, this movement taking off right now across the world, really, they're so proud of their slogan, "We are the 99 percent," I think it's bad marketing! I think they ought to say, "We are the 99.95% percent that don't have a voice inside of this government, because the government is so keenly attuned to the whispers of the 0.05%."

Elections Encourage Extortion

Lessig: So our system right now encourages a kind of political extortion, because members of Congress recognize that in a obvious way, they have certain benefits that they can hand out to to the public and the public should be grateful, and maybe even help pay for that. So the standard dynamic happens all the time in the context of taxes.

Tax code is filled with all of these temporary tax provisions, so as it's about to expire, a member can call up a company that benefits from that special tax benefit and say, "You know, we need support to make sure that we can get this tax benefit extended for another two years, and that's support is going to need to be really powerful and really strong," and that of course is a way to signal to that company that if they're not willing to step up and offer that support, maybe the congressman's not in a position to actually get that through. So members of Congress practice this behavior all the time, but the more interesting thing is, people in the business community experience it, as they've said in interviews again and again, as a kind of extortion. They recognize if they don't play the game, they're not going to get what they need.

Congress, a Farm League for K Street

Lessig: We have to recognize Congress has become a kind of farm league for K Street. K Street, of course, is where all the lobbyists work, and what that means is, people have this common business model where they imagine their life in government as a stepping stone to their life on K Street as a lobbyist. And if that's true, then these are not people who are about to change radically the way in which K Street functions, these are people who want to keep the system so that they have their nice exit to K Street after they're finished with Washington.

Nine percent of Americans have confidence in Congress. You just have to put that in context— nine percent, there were certainly more people who believed in the British crown at the time of the Revolution than who believe in this Congress today. So that level of confidence, I think, is at bankruptcy level, and when a nation or when a political system is bankrupt it needs to face that fact and fix itself. But I think that if we can get these different movements to recognize that there might actually be a common thing they agree about, so they don't have common ends, these two movements, but they might have a common enemy, and that common enemy is this corrupt system for funding our Congress.

This is a very diverse political nation and no side is going to legitimately capture the field and grab eighty percent of America on their views, and if that's true then and we do need eighty percent to make some substantial constitutional change, then we need to find a way to talk so that eighty percent could actually follow us.

A Republic, If You Can Keep It

Lessig: Benjamin Franklin was extremely old at the 1787 Constitutional Convention, barely able to participate, just sat there more from moral support than for any wisdom he could offer. He was being carried from the Convention and was stopped in the streets of Philadelphia by a woman who said to him, "Mr. Franklin, what have you wrought?" And Franklin said, "A republic, madam—if you can keep it."

So a republic, by which they meant a representative democracy, by which they intended a government dependent upon the people alone. We've lost that republic. And it's critical, I think, that we find a way to restore it and get it back.

CHAPTER 48

Three Years Later, What Has Come of Occupy Wall Street?

09/17/2014

This week marks the third anniversary of protesters descending on Wall Street to protest the havoc wrought by the 2008 Financial Meltdown, which had hit all Americans hard, except for the ones who had caused it.

What began as an open call from Adbusters to show up with a tent grew from dozens to hundreds, to thousands, to tens of thousands. Far from rejecting the extended sit-in, area businesses plied demonstrators with food and support. Those who could not make it to New York started their own hometown Occupy protests in solidarity, hundreds of them, across the country and around the world.

Adhering to the advertised mantra, "What is our one demand?" the Occupy activists connected with like-minded organizers in social justice and helped paint a portrait of the larger malfeasance plaguing society today: Bankers who had pushed derivatives industry-wide as a credible investment, while knowing they were bogus funds made of worthless mortgages, had led the stock and housing markets into a punishing recession, while using government bailouts to give themselves obscene bonuses despite their negligence.

At this same time was an emerging generation of unemployed millennials saddled with unprecedented student debt, as the banks had consolidated the student loan racket with high interest rates and no chance of bankruptcy protection under President Bush.

And who was looking out for Americans in this modern Depression? Basically, no one, because things got so bad in the first place because our elected leaders have become so beholden to their campaign donors. Since the 2010 Supreme Court decision Citizens United allowed unlimited outside spending in elections, candidates had dropped all pretense of serving their constituents, instead shifting their attention (and positions) in deference to billionaire kingmakers and Super PACs.

When beholding such a zero-sum option, it might seem clear why the only option left would be to get everyone you know to go out to the streets and bring this messed up paradox to the attention of everybody. Which is why, for whatever Occupy Wall Street is remembered for at its height, it should be considered an intervention for the country — a staged disruption by those who care, trying to alert an ailing entity to the damage it is inflicting. In this case, that entity with the destructive addictions is our modern political process, where who has the most money makes the rules, at the cost of all else — if it's a Texas fertilizer plant exploding near a school, a chemical company polluting drinking water for all of West Virginia, or gun manufacturers decrying regulations despite massacred children.

With that is mind, assessing the impact of Occupy Wall Street might be best done by considering the goals of those who camped out in Zuccotti Park. For one, this was a protest, not a political party, so comparisons to the Tea Party are like apples and oranges. While the Tea Party turned outrage at the government into electoral gains (with a lot of help and money from the Kochs), Occupy Wall Street was at the opposite end of the spectrum - the end of the spectrum that views officeholders as courtesans for the corporate class. Asking Occupy activists why they didn't just start a political party and run for office is like asking an atheist why they didn't just pray harder.

Another essential in gauging the importance of Occupy Wall Street is recognizing that the Occupy movement did not simply fizzle out or lose steam. The fact is, Occupy encampments were broken up in a coordinated effort led by the Department of Homeland Security working with local police departments. This coordination was reported by Jason Leopold after acquiring DHS documents through the Freedom of Information Act. Far from losing momentum, the Occupy presence had grown so intense nationwide, gaining sustained media coverage, that this had become the biggest threat to the status quo in modern times. In widely documented raids, police drove protesters from public lands with blunt force, tear gas, and arrest, then proceeded to blame Occupy protesters for the mess that was left behind. Young protesters sprayed in the face with pepper spray without warning or provocation, rubber bullets fired at peaceful demonstrators, police charging with batons, this is what oppression looked like in 2011. This marked the era of the militarized police force, which has come under scrutiny in the wake of the Ferguson PD's effort at martial law in Missouri.

So, besides the realization that heavily armed police forces consider themselves at war with their own communities, what else can we attribute to Occupy Wall Street with the benefit of hindsight? The immediate impact seemed to be how the debate in America changed almost overnight. No sooner had President Obama assumed office in 2009 than Republicans and conservatives began howling about deficit reduction. This sounds like a normal thing you do when you are running a first-world nation, but a more accurate way to look at it is that Republicans and Tea Partiers were demanding that Obama pay off the credit card charges from Bush/Cheney's trillion-dollar war, as well as their $2 trillion giveaway in taxes to the very rich. And they were acting like these bills arrived with the Obama family in the White House. Without fail, the mainstream media and Beltway punditry wrung their hands about what Obama was gong to do with this mess, that he better do something or we'd go off the fiscal cliff that John Boehner just made up, and it would be all Obama's fault that Boehner refused to hold a vote on basic government funding like every Congress before him.

But a funny thing happened when a few folks started talking about the richest one percent using their money to work the political system to get even richer. "WE ARE THE 99%" became the rallying cry of a generation. The simplicity and inclusivity was said to be worthy of Madison Avenue. At once the conversation had shifted, and in that discourse, a word started coming up that used to seem unspeakable: class. To at once dispel that American notion that we are so different from other countries while decrying staggering inequality made the struggle of others real. Not like a news piece on a family clipping coupons during a recession. Real, like this weighs on you, and becomes a sense of indignation for your fellow American, the way you were outraged when you saw New Orleans submerged from broken levees and its citizens struggling for days following Hurricane Katrina.

That awareness was more than a narrative, more than a meme, more than a point in a debate. The broad perception was that America wasn't just on the wrong track, it had been held up by railroad bandits.

What this really did was set the stage for the 2012 elections.

Through the drifting clouds of tear gas, stepping over the trampled bodies of demonstrators, and grinning into the same cameras that just showed all hell breaking lose, came Mr. Magoo, the most awe-inspiring tone-deaf candidate for president at the worst/best possible time. With Bain Capital affirming his vulture cred, an income so huge he refused to reveal his tax returns, he ran on absolutely nothing except saying what we have now isn't working, even though it seemed to be working fine for him.

This was the guy with his finger on the pulse of America who insisted, "Corporations are people, my friend," presumably thinking he was talking to a corporation. Corporate personhood had been a target of ire for Occupy Wall Street since it tends to indemnify financial criminals, and also because Citizens United had granted corporations VIP access to politicians. If Occupy Wall Street had been criticized for calling out how 1% of the people own 40% of the wealth, it sure seemed kinder than insisting that 47% of Americans would never take care of themselves and only live off of the government. When he lost by five million votes, he was the only one surprised, and blamed the weather.

But the disconnect was real, and continued. It seemed every few months there was another tortured outburst in print from some of the wealthiest men in Manhattan about how unfair the scorn was they faced, even though this was years after the protesters left Zuccotti. The people who seemed to be taking Occupy Wall Street the most seriously were the ones that it was intended for.

As I screen my documentary *PAY 2 PLAY,* I am asked sometimes what happened to Occupy, since it is included in our film about outsiders trying to have a voice in our political system. I will tell them about how I have met others at our screenings that preface their activism by saying they got motivated first from Occupy Wall Street. I met a young woman in Seattle who had mobilized first as a local Occupy organizer, who had since been elected to city council. Some of the very entities hosting our film about the problems with money in politics were off-shoots from local Occupy groups.

But I think more than anything, the point of Occupy was using your voice to speak out and finding out that you are not alone, there are many who feel the same way, and you are energized by this shared recognition. And once that common reality and strength is realized, you can go back to sleeping in bed and still live in accordance to your own mission.

Maybe someday we'll have a reunion for the Class of 2011. But for now, our gratitude and admiration go out to all who occupied and inspired. Thank you for showing us that we are not alone. Our patriotism and compassion will push this pay-to-play system into the dustbin of history.

The 2012 DNC

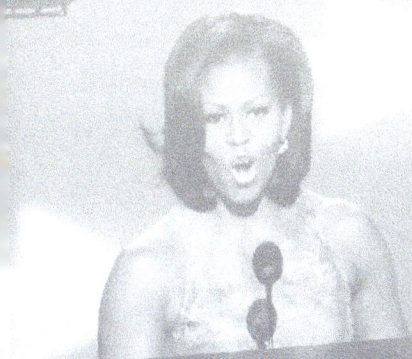

CHAPTER 49

Jodie Evans and Code Pink: The Art of Infiltration

09/12/2012

The political conventions have become a reliable playing field for protesters from all walks of life to gather outside the conventions where their voices won't be heard otherwise. This was most dramatically realized in 1968 at the DNC in Chicago, when over a million anti-war protesters descended on the streets of Chicago to face brutal violence by the Chicago Police, broadcast live.

As conventions have advanced, so have their security precautions, to where the conventions have become the testing ground of security and crowd control technologies, from the use of audio dispersal equipment in 2008, to the use of orange fence-like webbing to net crowds in 2004 during the RNC in New York City.

In 2012, however, there was not the protest presence that the conventions have come to expect. While the threat of Hurricane Issac kept many away from the RNC in Tampa, Fla., the DNC in Charlotte did not see the masses that have assembled in recent times. In 2004, upwards of a million people descended on New York to protest President George W. Bush and the Iraq War. In 2012, the protest population measured in the thousands.

Of course, this allows other groups to enjoy that much more of the spotlight. Code Pink has become the All-Star Team of convention demonstrations, from colorful fun protests outside to fearless disruptions inside. I interviewed Code Pink co-founder Jodie Evans about Code Pink's role in dissent at the conventions, the response to their tactics, and the state of protest in 2012.

What does the infiltration process entail?

Evans: Both the RNC and DNC want desperately to keep us out of the conventions. So we go out and find out who's upset with those parties and want to share their credential with us, because they don't have the courage to disrupt but they want us to disrupt with our message. And in Tampa it was easy, because the Ron Paul delegates were pretty pissed and they were, as soon as they saw us, they were like, "Here's our credential!" But it's very hard to get a credential because people don't want to lose their access and people who have given us their credentials in the past have been denied their credentials for the next convention. So it's very locked-down about other people getting in, and so we've got to use all our charms to get that credential to get inside.

What kind of response do you get?

Evans: At the RNC, when I was standing in there with my message about Wisconsin and Scott Walker, nobody booed, they didn't even interrupt anything I was saying. They were just looking, and because I can go with a fresh message, they were trying to figure out what it meant. The next day, at Romney and Ryan, the whole audience gets up, tries to block you, and tries to cover the message with their own messaging, "USA, USA!"

The last night, there were four Code Pinkers that got in for Romney, and people around them pulled them down to the ground, and pulled on tight really hard, and it causes quite a ruckus, the ruckus pulls more cameras in that direction to show that there's a disruption. But at the same time, Ray and Medea got hurt.

Last night [at the DNC] the message we took in was around the drones, no drones in Afghanistan killing innocent people. No one said anything. Ray was there for I think around four minutes holding the banner and talking. She said, "I got tired of talking, I felt I was being rude." And no one disrupted, no one said, "Shut up," and the cop that escorted her out said, "Thank you very much." And he held the banner for her on the way out. A lot of people as she was walking out said thank you, and we noticed on our Twitter feed as people were responding they said, "Thank you."

I always think that what we do at Code Pink is, we stand up in the middle of the lie and tell another story so that people have a chance to make another decision, instead of being force-fed something. And that started out with the name Code Pink, so instead of Bush trying to frighten us with code red, code orange, code yellow, we said Code Pink for peace, which was to expose that violence and the way they were trying to create fear.

But you know, when I disrupted Bush when he was in the middle of his acceptance speech in 2004 in New York, that made national media, and I can't tell you how many people have come out and said, "That changed my life, I was working in Wall Street." That woman is now running

Environment California. They realized they they could be using their voice, this was frustrating to them and the thing to do is to get up and do something about it. And like Laura, our intern, who disrupted Ryan in Tampa, she's never disrupted before. And a New York Times reporter said, "So why did you do that?" She said, "Some young woman like me will know to use her voice, not necessarily to disrupt the nominee for vice president at the Republican National Convention, but she'll have the courage to use her voice.

That's a lot of we do. When we're in the middle of so much, so much manipulation and contortion of what is true, that we stand up in the middle of that and say, "There's another fact that you're missing," or "That's a lie!" We've taken to painting giant pink slips that said "Bush, you lie, you should be fired!" We're bringing another story into the room.

What do you think of the protests this year in Charlotte?

Evans: When we started Code Pink, that's now almost ten years ago, we were with thousands of people in the streets. Our march before Bush went to war with Iraq, we had 10,000 women marching in pink towards the White House, and they had blocked the White House like they've never had before, 'cause of course women are more frightening than anything.

And here [Charlotte], when there is so much being...I mean, we're being raped and robbed and violated and you know, everything is wrong with this democracy, what should be a democracy but isn't, and it's just, the chilling effect is frightening. And I think you hear that, what's happening on the stage at the Democratic Convention. They're feeling the chilling effect too, and everything is about getting people engaged to mass vote because they also feel the chilling effect. I remember this back in you know, after '68, the chilling effect, the death of Martin Luther King.

I remember that sense of the chilling effect and I don't know why it's happening now. The arrests at Occupy, does that frighten people? What has people watching what's happening and not using this voice at all? [Democrats] wouldn't be working so hard to get everybody engaged if they were engaged, because they're having the same experience we are. That's what this convention is about. They're feeling the apathy too. I don't think that the issues being engaged, because they're not talking about a lot of the issues that affect people. They're talking about getting back to the middle class, they are not talking about what's not working. They're talking about what's working and trying to inspire you.

So I don't know if people who would think as activists feel like they're being addressed. Matter of fact, I've run into many of them and they're frustrated and they feel like it's a reality television show. And they're working on, what happens after the election? Or they're working on, how do we get our base engaged? Because the other is so frightening. When you don't hold them accountable, they just get pompous and arrogant. We have let them get away with murder for so long. I mean, this is Rove.

Even if 99% of the people are against something, the policy doesn't change until the money changes. So we all come out of activism in the 60's and 80's around so many things. But now people are really feeling it doesn't matter.

And that's why we keep doing it. Because if you don't even speak it, it really gets to have power.

What is the story of this convention here in Charlotte?

Evans: I would say that the Democrats knew that they they had a PR problem, a relationship problem, and inspiration problem, and they pulled out all the stops to do what they could to get voters to see the difference between the Republicans and them. To address the places that the Republicans have tried to pull the rug out straight on and at least give people a choice.

CHAPTER 50

The People's Convention

09/06/2012

Where the conventions were once a confluence of ideas, it's no secret they have come to strive for spectacle, turning earnest debates for improving the quality of life for Americans into platitudes. But the opportunity that the conventions have come to embody is the assembly outside the official proceedings, where people from across the country have gathered who are as passionate as the attendees, if not more.

A rousing forum for discourse, speeches, music, and inspiration was at Progressive Central, hosted at a local church outside Uptown by Progressive Democrats of America. Moderated by the acclaimed commentator for *The Nation*, John Nichols, the "People's Convention" ran down the list of how the Progressive movement could achieve its goals of Medicare for All, ending the wars abroad, rebuilding the labor movement, and fighting the influence of money in politics.

Throughout the day at Progressive Central, speakers like Rep. Keith Ellison (D-MN) and Rep. Jim McGovern (D-MA) expressed their hopes for what a second Obama term could bring to the progressive agenda. McGovern and former Governor Mike Dukakis both attested to Mitt

Romney's abysmal term as Governor of Massachusetts. McGovern stressed why Romney didn't run for a second term, because he was so unpopular. Dukakis reiterated that under Romney, Massachusetts was 47th out of 50 for job creation.

The most colorful display was with folk rock duo Emma's Rebellion and their background dancers, members of Code Pink dressed as Vaginas, who were well-covered at the RNC. The song "Take Your Vagina to the RNC" brought the house down.

But it was the poignant acceptance of an award from PDA by the esteemed Rep. John Conyers, who has been in Congress so long he worked on the Voting Rights Act, that was the highlight. Conyers told the audience that the resistance and pressure facing Obama is greater than any Democrat he had ever seen.

John Nichols spoke in interview about what he thought the story of this year's Democratic convention was — Obama's opportunity to do more than just hit the right political notes, but to convince the larger population to deliver a mandate for the president who brought the Affordable Care Act to them as just a start of what's possible.

What is the story of this convention?

Nichols: I think the biggest story of the convention, obviously, is whether President Obama will use this opportunity not to merely seek re-election, but to seek the kind of victory that we've seen in the best of circumstances from progressive Democratic presidents in the past. And the classic example is Roosevelt in 1936. Franklin Roosevelt didn't just run for re-election, he ran to get a governing majority so that he could actually do something. And that's a critical thing in any rougher effort to achieve a second term. Presidents can run for a second term in a pointless way—get it and simply serve out their last four years and they might often win in that circumstance.

But what you really look for are those rare moments where a president runs for re-election with a message, with a vision, and this is the point at which to state it. President Obama has many great strengths, I have a good deal of admiration in many areas, but I have not seen him always be the boldest of players. And so this is really a test…If he gets up there and really sculpts out a vision, I think there's a possibility that he would not only be re-elected but I might bring in a Congress that could do something. If, on the other hand, it is a rather more traditional, somewhat forgettable speech, as well as all the other elements of the convention, then I think we're in for, frankly, the sort of desultory fall election that we often have. You know, Democrats and voters and yelling at each other yelling at each other but not a lot coming out of it.

I think Barack Obama will probably win—and this is a remarkable thing in and of itself, because the amount of money that is being brought into this process is so immense, that simply to beat the money is amazing thing. But again, I think it's important to think about what happens when you beat the money, do you beat it simply for the purpose of winning an election? Or do you beat it with a purpose of extending a vision of doing something profound? And it's at this convention where we'll figure out whether he's going to do something profound.

CHAPTER 51

As He Returns to Prison, Don Siegelman Still Seeks Justice

09/11/2012

Today I received an email from Dana Siegelman, sharing her sad situation—she was about to drive 485 miles to take her father, the former Governor of Alabama, to prison.

In a labyrinthine epic that would make Kafka blush, Don Siegelman has spent the past 13 years ensnared in a legal battle that has seen trumped-up corruption charges, unapologetic partisan prosecutions and his governorship stolen out from under him in the middle of the night.

On Tuesday, September 11, 2012, Don Siegelman returns to federal prison to face six and a half years for a conviction over his appointment to a non-profit organization of someone who had previously donated to his campaign. The innocuousness of a donor and an appointee being the same person in any city, state, or federal office notwithstanding, laws at the time in Alabama had been set so that the bar was so low so as to not be able to convict

250

anyone of *quid pro quo* corruption, if their case were brought to a jury. Many legal experts and pundits across the spectrum have since decried this legal interpretation used in the case of Don Siegelman.

But that was only the beginning. Don Siegelman saw his re-election as Alabama's governor vanish in the thick of the night, when one suspect county reallotted its votes enough to swing the election. It should be noted that at each of these junctures, the key players in Siegelman's travails are all close colleagues with Karl Rove. That Rove's fingerprints are all over this case has not so much been disputed, but rather ignored by the media and mainstream outlets, as Siegelman faces an unrepentant federal judge in Alabama who will not let Siegelman's case be resolved. After a dozen years and a fortune in legal fees, Siegelman's only hope lies now with a pardon from President Barack Obama, who has largely avoided taking on Rove's legacy of misdeeds.

At Progressive Central in Charlotte during the DNC, I was fortunate enough to meet Gov. Siegelman, and he afforded me the time for this exclusive interview in advance of his return to prison.

What's the status of your case?

Siegelman: The case has gone through the full set of Appeals. And we're kind of caught in a Catch-22, because the trial judge and I had a political battle ten years ago. The presiding judge of the 11th Circuit Court of Appeals is the former client of Karl Rove who helped steal the election by illegally certifying the votes and stopping the recount. So I'm not able to get normal relief under the electoral or judicial system and so that's why we're calling on our friends to go to change.org/pardondon or donsiegelman.org and go online and sign a petition to President Obama asking him to either pardon me or to commute my sentence.

Why do you think people have a problem accepting election fraud?

Siegelman: As young Americans, we're brought up in pledging allegiance to the flag, singing "The Star-Spangled Banner," and having respect for the country and our justice system. We want to believe that this country is a leader of the free world and that we're promoting democracy and civil rights and human rights and so it's very difficult for the average citizen to conclude that we would use torture as a means of interrogation, or that we would be led into war under false pretenses, or that we would use the Department of Justice as a vehicle to win elections. And so it's hard for people to come to grips with abuse of power by their own government.

Tell me about some of the support you've received.

Siegelman: Well, we've had we've really had tremendous support from all over the country, all over the world, in fact, and it continues to grow by the day. I'm very blessed to have supporters, not only, you know, on the streets, but also in Congress, people like John Conyers, which brings me here today to the Progressive Democrats of America rally and also to this convention to say thank you to people like steady warriors Linda Sanchez and Debbie Wasserman-Schultz and others who've been very supportive of my case, very understanding of the situation in which I find myself.

What's the next legal turn for you?

Siegelman: Well, as a practical matter, really, the only thing that is available is the President either commuting my sentence or issuing a pardon. We've got a couple of appeals but they both have to go through the 11th Circuit, and that, you know, I wouldn't want to pin my hopes on those legal appeals.

What's Enterprise, Alabama?

Siegelman: Enterprise, Alabama, is the home of the judge [Mark Everrett Fuller], it's also the home of his bread and butter, which is a defense contracting company called Doss Aviation. It was interesting that he's built his business over time, primarily relying on his contacts in Congress and in the U.S. Senate, people who have been on the Appropriations Committee or Armed Services Committee. His namesake, Terry Everett, was a congressman from South Alabama, from Duncan, just the next the next county down. But during the course of the trial, he was notified by the government that he was up for a two hundred million dollar a year contract and was subsequently, at the end of the trial, given that contract. So, two hundred million-dollar contract per year, renewable for five years, I believe.

As you face another stretch in prison, what keeps you going?

Siegelman: Well, the hope and belief that the truth will come out, and that, not only will I be exonerated and given my freedom, but you know, be given a chance to help impact the criminal justice system in the future for others. What this has done for me is to help me understand that this is not something that is an isolated case but that is something that's very pervasive, has happened to a lot of people, and is going to happen to a lot of people unless we balance the scales of justice to make our process more fair. And that is my hope for the Obama administration after 2012.

CHAPTER 52

Dana Siegelman: My Dad the Political Prisoner

Inside the DNC, Don Siegelman's daughter Dana happened to see, of all people, Karl Rove. She says that he made eye contact with her, and as soon as she confronted him, he lashed out at her, and even started pointing his finger in her face accusingly. The more frequent outbursts like this from Rove are telling that his many efforts to dodge subpoenas, indictments, and lingering investigations seem to be taking its toll on the campaign adviser/Super PAC fundraiser.

Dana Siegelman shared her story with Current TV immediately after her confrontation with the man who has made her father's career of public service a Sisyphean hell. After meeting Dana Siegelman at the DNC, I filmed and edited this interview of her for an appeal video on her father's behalf.

* * *

Dana Siegelman: According to everyone who's ever worked for Dad, he was the hardest working governor or politician they'd ever worked for. He would wake up at four o'clock and he'd have already shot off the emails for the day by five, and everyone had about 15 emails in their inbox from him. And he would make time for having breakfast with his children before he ran off to work, wake us up at like 6:30, we'd have breakfast at seven, he dropped us off, and those were special times. I had more quality time with Dad because he was acutely aware of his busy schedule, so when he made time for us, it was really time for us and it was wonderful. So that, for the four years that he was governor, my most special moments were having breakfast in the morning with him.

Then I do remember the night of the election in 2002. We were just like, "Is Dad gonna win?! What's going to happen?" and he won! And we thought—we were in our pajamas—we thought, "we have to go down there and support our Dad!" So we begged Security, "Please, take us back, we want to go on stage!" So we got dressed and ran on stage and surprised Dad as he, you know, said thank you, to the state of Alabama for re-electing him.

And the next morning, around four o'clock, he got a phone call from someone saying, "Bob Riley is claiming that he won the election, and some votes were found in Baldwin county, and you're going to have to contest this."

He just wanted to recount. He wanted to know how the votes were really cast. And he asked the Attorney General at the time, "Let's have a recount," and this guy said, "Anyone who dares recounting votes is going to go to prison. I will jail anyone who tries to count these votes."

So he conceded nicely, he said, "You know, I know I'm not going to win in the courts. The courts are Republican. I understand that I really don't have a chance. So I'm going to run again in four years. It's not a problem." And after he announced that he was running again, he was indicted for bribery. For appointing a man to a health board, a non-paying board he had presided on for 12 years under three other governors. He didn't even want the position, they had to say, you know, please come back.

They were able to get a Bush-friendly judge, someone who had been appointed by George W. Bush, his name is Mark Everett Fuller. And what's interesting about Mark Fuller is that he was District Attorney before my dad was Governor and had corrupted the District Attorney's Office.

And the person my dad replaced him with, Gary McWillie, actually brought a case against Judge Fuller: you spiked the salary of your chief investigative officer, you corrupted the office and used it for political purposes, basically they won their case against mark fuller even as he was a judge at the time. Four years later, he's presiding judge over my father's case.

What makes matters worse is, this federal judge also had vetted economic interest in the Bush Administration. Why? He owned a company called Doss Aviation which refueled plains, trained pilots, provided soldiers' uniforms. And he was a rewarded by the Bush administration with a $200 million defense contract.

So during the course of this trial, Mark Fuller was pretty much going through a divorce. He had been having an affair with his clerk for about five years. And there's a lot of people that feel that that is enough information to issue a new trial. Mark Fuller was always and very happily one-sided. Never rebuke the jury for falling asleep. I mean, when I was there, half the jury was asleep.

It was a long deliberation. They were deliberating like, three days. And from what I understand, he threatened the jury during deliberation, saying, in a paraphrase "You know I can keep you here till next Christmas I need a verdict."

And immediately after, within hours of the judge saying that, they had a conviction.

In 2007, Dad was sentenced to seven years and dragged away, literally, in handcuffs and shackles, leg manacles, to a maximum security prison in Atlanta where he was put in solitary confinement.

I didn't get to talk to my dad for two months. I was petrified. I didn't want to go out in public. I didn't want to speak to people. I was really depressed. I would cry myself to sleep at night, praying for him, asking that I would take any fear that he had, I'd have it for myself, because I didn't want him to suffer. And I knew that he was—my dad's spirit is so strong. He's such a positive person that he only said positive things when I was finally able to talk to him. He assured me, everything is fine, I'm totally fine, he never let on for a minute that he had suffered. Because he didn't want his children, his family, his friends, to worry.

You know, the appeal process, it basically ends before it starts. We were sending all of the appeals to the Eleventh Circuit Court of Appeals in Atlanta. And the Chief Justice was…he was the same man who refused a recount to my father in Alabama. He is now the Chief Justice over the Eleventh Circuit Court of Appeals, where all of Dad's appeals go.

The Supreme Court refused to hear the case, sent it back to Judge Fuller without comment, basically saying, do what you will with this person, who you absolutely hate. A huge injustice has occurred.

There's a woman, Jill Simpson, Dana Jill Simpson, who just two weeks I think after Dad was taken to prison said, "I was involved in this and I have to say something," and she offered up an affidavit. What was really shocking is

Karl Rove's role in directing the Department of Justice not just to target Don Siegelman, but to target Democrats.

Hopefully Dad will be released. Unprecedented, I know, via presidential pardon. Five years ago, when Dad was dragged away in handcuffs and shackles, I felt completely alone and vulnerable and I wanted to hide. I wanted to throw the covers over my head and isolate myself from any further damage. Fast forward five years, the anger that I feel was not the same that I felt before. It was not full of fear, it was full of love for my dad, and the sense that I will not stand to be buried under this injustice.

PART EIGHT

The Culture Wars

CHAPTER 53

Drug Testing for Welfare Recipients?

03/07/2009

I would like to wholeheartedly endorse the movement to mandate drug tests for welfare recipients. I know that many might disagree with me, but I think it is the only responsible thing to do.

After all, aren't these freeloaders given our tax dollars? Shouldn't we know if they are harming themselves, and affecting their judgment? Plus, once someone takes America's money, they accept being judged by other Americans. And I am sure we all disapprove of this kind of drug abuse.

Exactly how high were the welfare recipients at AIG, Citi Group, Lehman Brothers, Merrill Lynch, GM, and Bank of America? Based on their judgment and lack of responsibility, the clinical diagnosis would be "really fucking high."

But high on what, exactly? We as a nation need to determine these dangerous substances to prevent future relapses in economic judgment. While the glib insulation of these captains of industry might suggest being stoned on some hydroponic kush or similar strain of Indica, their actions of chasing bad money with our money show the combative yet clueless character of college kids swilling Jagermesiter, or Mickey Rourke in Barfly.

However, the manic pace at which these welfare recipients raced through their bailout monies to pimp out their offices while millions of Americans struggle under their ruinous financial management seems to convincingly indicate that they were all as coked up as Al Pacino before he got gunned down in *Scarface*.

Yet, to look at many of these investment strategies — such as pushing default-ready loans as a commodity to every investor in the world, or building overpriced cars that run on 10 MPG — it suggests that these Rand-ian geniuses were blotto on blotter paper, tripping balls and looking at investment portfolios make groovy patterns as they spiral downward. Timothy Leary might well have been a Keynesian economist ahead of his time.

Until the Treasury Department demands drug tests of every single employee of these "Too Big To Fail" businesses (guess what—they failed), we will not know what was driving these enriched, inebriated decision makers. Their euphoric holiday spending with money meant to stable the American and International economies were likely influenced by MDMA (ecstasy), although there have not been reports of AIG traders dancing like pricks.

I recognize that the intention in legislation of drug testing welfare recipients was targeted at poor people who could not really afford drugs (however much they might appreciate the levity), because Republicans seem to have no problem telling people unable to speak for themselves how they should live their life.

As such, in response to the many concerned conservatives about CEO's being robbed of their bonus bounty—even if it is rewarding catastrophic failure the likes of which human civilization has not seen before—I believe that this approach will be considered fair.

If a welfare mother raising a couple of kids on her own while trying to work is held to such high standards of a drug-free life for receiving hundreds of dollars a month in government assistance, then obviously it stands to reason that someone receiving 1000 times the government money should be held one thousand times more personally responsible for their actions and behavior.

Were these titans of industry abusing psychiatric prescriptions? Should somebody have been making sure they were taking their medication? Perhaps every-day anti-depressants should be stepped up to anti-psychotics, or something hardcore like Lithium to treat the bipolar disorder of megalomaniacal bankers who demand flush compensation for undermining the economy of what was the last superpower in the world.

There seems to be a disconnect today on the Right, where government intervention into poor people's lives, Third World countries, civil liberties, gay couples, wombs everywhere, and the washed up industries of their donors is necessary and right—yet any government oversight on how its money is spent is wrong, helping home-owners mired in the same mortgage mess as the bankers draws self-righteous losers ranting, and jump-starting the D.O.A. economy is hysterically labeled "Socialism" by millions of people who do not even know what it actually means and how far off we actually are from it. (Hint: Socialism is like the opening of every *Star Wars* movie: "A long time ago, in a galaxy far, far away...")

Perhaps much wider drug testing will be needed.

CHAPTER 54

Missing the Point of
Atlas Shrugged

05/11/2009

Much has been made of Ayn Rand's opus of late, *Atlas Shrugged*, and its relevance to our current economic crisis.

To condense a thousand page novel into a lede: As the U.S. worsens, captains of industry disappear, creating a secret utopian community of their own led by John Galt, waiting to return into society until it crumbles so badly without them, the lights of New York go dark.

To condense a thousand page allegory on Objectivism into a rationale: Some people are just geniuses, and they should be left alone to produce, because their ingenuity is what allows society to flourish. Intrusion into their process is oppression.

The inherent problem of literature is that often times citing it is in itself an appearance of wisdom, superior reasoning, of being right. And as grandiose as the grunting of "Going Galt" by conservatives has been, their many detractors have disparaged an otherwise good novel.

As long-winded as the book is, it has a cool story, and through bringing the reader into the minds of leading industrialists, it captivates the imagination and lets us fantasize about the prestige, power, and ability of being a genius in the world that Ayn Rand divines from a familiar United States in the middle of the last century.

In the heightened reality of her universe, there are the geniuses, whose innovations benefit all of us eventually, and there are the looters (haters), untalented bureaucrats who restrain the geniuses through repetitive mandates requiring their successes be shared with the government to make up for its lack of innovation. The role of the government in her book is as cartoonish as her antagonists.

It is a thousand-paged stacked deck. Ayn Rand's portrait of America is as rarefied as Norman Rockwell's.

The danger is that through reading this novel, many people become so empathetic to the heroic geniuses that they begin to believe that they are themselves geniuses. (After all, they just got through a preachy thousand-page book.)

HINT: If you needed this book to realize you are a genius, then you are not a genius.

Thus, the empty threat of defection to a non-existent utopia is proffered by people who would not be eligible for said utopia.

To brag of being Galt-ian, you may as well brag about being Vulcan. Both offer some practical wisdom from their respective fictitious worlds — but why not wear funny ears while you're at it?

There is another inherent flaw with the principle that an unencumbered genius will perform for the betterment of society. That same naiveté fed Alan Greenspan, star of Ayn Rand's salon of sophists, who as Fed Chief reasoned that traders and corporations would not put out flawed products, funds or services, because to do so would obviously be of detriment to their future sustainability. The Free Market would thus be a noble marketplace where competition keeps its players serving the consumers.

This blind trust in some gentlemen's code that does not exist allowed the rampant run up of short-sighted scroungers to swindle millions of Americans through predatory lending, inflated mortgage securities, Enron, Big Pharma, and the insidious hold the oil industry has on our government and society.

Now, even Alan Greenspan is calling for nationalizing banks. Poor Ayn must be spinning in her solid gold sarcophagus.

Her life was like her lordly literature. Born in St. Petersburg, her family was uprooted by the Russian revolution of 1917 and her father's business seized by looters. (I think it would behoove many of the people crying out about socialism that Ayn Rand's idea of socialism is the real deal, when Lenin was leading mobs in the streets and Bolsheviks were taking your stuff away from you.) At 21, she came to America on a visa to visit relatives, never to return to Russia. (Anti-Immigration zealots who revere Ayn Rand, take note, you champion an illegal Russian immigrant, who was also a devout atheist.)

On her second day in Los Angeles, she was discovered by Hollywood titan Cecil B. DeMille, who saw her peering through the gates of a studio lot, and then hired her to become an extra and eventually a script reader (no doubt because he recognized her true genius at 21). She met her future movie star husband on the lot a week later.

While married, she famously had an open affair with her protege, even naming an heroic character after him in *Atlas Shrugged*. This heir apparent to Objectivism, Nathaniel Branden, was also married, and in their erudite circle of being objective to what Ayn Rand wanted, Branden's wife and Rand's husband had to be cool with them boning.

But when Ayn Rand found out that her boy toy was objectively screwing a young actress acolyte of theirs, she went ballistic, ostracizing him from the institute he had built for her, and bashing him in their literary journals without acknowledgment of their affair (actually pre-dating MySpace).

While a thinker cannot always be held to the ideals they author as inspiration to others, Ayn Rand in particular does not make a good role model. Actually, she was kind of a bitch. (I only dare say that because she's dead and can't get me.) When she died, her body was displayed next to a huge floral arrangement of the dollar sign, a symbol she lauded as the ultimate icon for the self.

As extreme as it might sound to worship a symbol of currency, self-empowerment and self-enrichment are hardly enemies of the American character. The individual's freedom is what our renegade country was founded on, and there is no threat to an American's rights (not counting the Bush years). There are in fact industries devoted to selling such success through books far easier to read than *Atlas Shrugged*. The lofty ideal of rational self-interest challenges the principle of personal responsibility, and lays the groundwork to rationalize anything.

This argument from a senior fellow at the Ayn Rand Institute sets the record straight on the recent rampant citing of *Atlas Shrugged*.

"If we are our brother's keeper, as Obama declares (echoing the conventional wisdom) — if your moral duty is to serve your neighbor and anyone else who is in need, then you don't have the moral right to pursue your own life and happiness."

Astonishingly, one actually can have compassion for other people and not thereby be enslaved.

The reference point for such a defensive assault on compunction is from an individual who did not want to feel culpable of compassion, and so has constructed a critique of others who are.

Any belief system can be used to justify one's means — but Ayn Rand's Objectivism is *about* justifying one's means.

CHAPTER 55

With Release of Rand Movie, a Rise in Rants on Reason

04/12/2011

I awoke the other day to this email from a stranger:

Just saw your 2009 piece on Atlas Shrugged. *You completely missed the point of Rand's book, which is that you can't consume what you don't produce, but that a lot of folks would like to consume what they can take from others. I'm looking forward to the movie next month. No doubt we will see the leftists out in force to tell us how bad it is. The best thing for* Atlas Shrugged *and Ayn Rand has been the Obama administration.*

I replied: "Then you can't see the movie if you didn't produce it, by that reasoning..."

A movie adaptation of any lengthy book is bound to reduce its ideas, themes, and arguments to piece meal phrases that will not do justice to the author's intent. But I foresee a particular risk in this upcoming film effort tackling Rand's opus of ego, and spurring some to further reduce it to clichés about how everyone is always trying to take your sh*t from you.

271

As it is, Ayn Rand's 1957 epic has enjoyed a revival among those who obsess that Obama is striving to subjugate them (hint: it's the corporations, not the government). Look at Nick Newcomen, an acolyte of Ayn that last year drove all over America to correspond to GPS coordinates so that his epic road trip would spell out on a map "READ AYN RAND" like terrestrial sky-writing.

People carve reason to fit their rationale. Ayn Rand's gospel of self-empowerment reads perilously close to selfishness justified by selfishness. As I maintained in my previous piece on *Atlas Shrugged*, there is a lot of brilliance in Rand's writing. So brilliant, it tends to blind readers into empathy with its persecuted geniuses, and let many readers feel they, too, are like the genius characters in Rand's tale. After all, they just got through a thousand-page book— that's like reading the Bible, or James Joyce, or the dictionary.

However, the narrative universe in Rand's saga of society unraveling is, from a literary standpoint, science fiction, written in the style of a melodrama, and riddled with repetition. Ideologically, it's a thousand-page stacked deck. Inspiring though it may be, the simplistic, black-and-white world in *Atlas Shrugged* is like an Art Deco-era *Star Wars*. The key difference — people aren't trying to run Jedis for Congress.

Ayn Rand waxes at length on how some people (geniuses) are better than others (looters), and her characters say the same things to each other over and over in different long-winded ways. I can't help but wonder: What kind of person has to do this? What did she have to convince herself of? Why do the characters speak to each other in essays?

Where many try to find ties to today's U.S. government in Ayn Rand's writing, it can be forgotten what her reference point really was. Born Alisa Zinov'yevna Rosenbaum, her family suffered their business being confiscated under the 1917 Russian Revolution by Lenin's Bolsheviks. Her idea of "the socialists are coming to get you" wasn't affordable health care — it was, literally: the socialists are coming to get you.

As I have maintained, I ultimately enjoyed the book and was drawn to parts of its driving philosophy. I recognized early on in the piece that the author had a bitter complaint against all the people trying to stifle innovation all the time, and figured she would cite examples from the real world, but she only showed it in her two-dimensional foils.

Ayn Rand prizes reason above all else. The problem is, even objective reasoning tends to be used subjectively. The nobility of reason as the penultimate approach to life over faith and compassion vanishes once exaggeration is injected into the argument process.

Any deviation from the accurate facts, devolved of emotion or selective recognition, betrays the virtue of reason. Exaggeration is frequently employed these days to turn a talking point into a terrifying call to arms. Embellishing your argument to incite fear in others so that they subscribe to your point of view is manipulating your case to gain more support, under a misrepresented pretense. Exaggeration is lying. Exaggeration should be recognized as the enemy of reason.

It's not that reason is so objectionable. It's what often passes for reason that is not only disingenuous, but insulting, and ultimately dangerous. Rand's encouragement of relying on labels for types of people, from looters to leftists, breeds oversimplification. Labels are another shortcut around reasoning, a short-sighted fallacy reduced to a descriptor trying to be passed off as accepted fact.

But ultimately, Ayn Rand put her own ego above everything else, not reason. She never again spoke to her contemporary conservative William F. Buckley after he quoted someone else's line of criticism of *Atlas Shrugged*. This is the author of the greatest selling novel of all time, as William F. Buckley pointed out to Charlie Rose.

Another act of her contempt to those who didn't give her absolute reassurance: Rand tore down her protégé and lover Nathaniel Branden (who she kept in an open arrangement between both their spouses) once she learned that he had slept with one of his own acolytes in their institute of objectivism. Her assaults in print against him failed to include her personal relations with him. To not acknowledge a jealous rage as a factor in the reasoning of the trouncing of a colleague before your shared followers — this defies the pretense of one's reasoning being superior to another.

When used selectively as a pretense, to be lauded as sublime because of verbose language suggesting superiority, Ayn Rand's principle of reason bears little distinction from the malleable rules behind any other religious belief system — ones that are always self-sustaining, that won't tolerate doubters and that tend to favor the predispositions of the leaders making the rules.

The problem of selective reasoning extends beyond literary blather into real world troubles when self-appointed acolytes of Ayn Rand inject her simplistic self-righteousness into things like the budget of the United States of America.

Rep. Paul Ryan, who has professed his adoration of Ayn, has touted a budget proposal that prolongs debt payoff, lowers taxes on the rich, and which the Nobel prize winning economist Paul Krugman referred to as a unicorn hunt. One of Ayn's most ardent admirers was Former Fed Chief Alan Greenspan, who was enamored with the ideas of unregulated markets to let geniuses thrive for the betterment of society. Why would the wise men of Wall Street cut corners and subvert the market — which would only strangle our economy and end up looking bad?

Surely the wealthiest tycoons wouldn't be so obsessed with bleeding our economy for a little more money. It's not like they would listen to their superior sense of self and rationalize selling predatory mortgage loans as derivatives on the international market, right? They certainly wouldn't endeavor in such fraud as boasting false ratings, used to coax the elderly into seemingly safe investments. They are successful, therefore they are geniuses, and therefore we as a society rely on their accomplishments to move us all forward. It stands to reason.

Because of course, all ambitious business leaders would share the same priorities of unabated self as Ayn Rand and Alan Greenspan, and the rules regulating industries exist only because whoever wrote them were looters (or as we might think of them today, "haters.")

Speaking of which, why do we even have traffic laws? Surely drivers are all looking out for the betterment of society, and they know that if they abuse the system by speeding or not waiting at intersections, there will eventually just be a pile up, and then the government would have to come bail them out. Those fast drivers wouldn't be reckless, because they know it might look bad for them later.

They're just geniuses for going so fast — they deserve even less regulation.

And because I insist I reached this ban on traffic laws through reason — sweet sacred reason! — who are you to tell me I'm wrong? You're just a looter trying to thwart my progress because you're jealous and want me to drive you everywhere since I decided that traffic laws don't apply to me. After all — it's me we're talking about here!

This is the inherent paradox in taking an absolutism about reason: if you arch to support any one person, book, or movie adaptation you haven't seen yet as further proof to your own prearranged beliefs, you are avoiding reason altogether. You are looking for gospel to buttress your faith. You are seeking repetition of ideas — fundamentally, the faulty premise that everything literally comes down to one side versus the other.

The idea that sides must be chosen in advance of the release of the film *Atlas Shrugged* feels a little like Team Jacob and Team Edward. With the look of a TV movie, I doubt that the "leftists" will be out in force telling Rand fans how bad the movie it is. Whoever would identify themselves as "Leftists" are likely preoccupied with the GOP's use of government to assault unions, state workers, pregnant women, teachers, the elderly, the ground, the skies, and the oceans, to worry about another science fiction movie that won't be as good as the book.

CHAPTER 56

Is *Dukes of Hazzard* Really Racist?

07/03/2015

The controversy and soul-searching surrounding TV Land's removal of *Dukes of Hazzard* reruns from its schedule has prompted concerns across social media along the lines of, "Is this going too far?" More than once, I have seen people question, "What's next?" with a list of other things that might be prone to "revisionism."

I figured this day would come, where we would look back on a beloved show from childhood and minimize the implications from the Confederate flag on their car. Because in many ways, it echoes what we hear Southerners say in their defense of the flag: This is what we grew up with, but it wasn't being used to advance racism or slavery at that time, it was more like a local flag. But because we grew up with it, it's sentimental, it's tradition, it reflects the pride of my people. (A lot of people grew up with segregation, too.)

That day turned out to be the massacre at the African Methodist Episcopal Church in Charleston, S.C., carried out coldly with expressed racist, terrorist objectives by a Confederate flag waver and selfie addict. The avowed white supremacy articulated at length by the shooter, plus his hopes for igniting a race war, kind of gave up the ghost on what that "Battle Flag" really meant and symbolized: actual

277

battle. The arguments did not fly this time around that the Confederate flag and its cause were about "Northern aggressors" or economics, since so many of the writings from the Civil War are now just clicks away, and apparently nobody bothered to give any other reasons at that time besides slavery.

But what does this have to do with a 35-year-old TV show? Honestly, probably not much. I can almost see the meetings at CBS back in the day, "How do we make them look Southern?" "A banjo, some shots of moonshine jugs, overalls?" "What about a Confederate flag? Those folks in the South never got over the war." "Great idea! We can even call the car 'The General Lee'!"

And here is where the idea of any unintentional association starts to seem a little more like a boner for the South to rise again. Obviously, the car was the show. They went through like 80 cars doing the stunts for that show, because of course cars don't keep driving after jumping a river. Kids across America knew and thought General Lee was cool, not really knowing anything about who he was or that he sent thousands to their deaths to keep black people enslaved. The car could have had an American flag, a Spirit of '76 emblem, or some pin-up girl, it really would not have mattered to the rest of the show. The car did jumps, spin-outs, chases — everyone can get behind a bright orange '69 Dodge Charger spitting out dirt from its roaring wheels, no matter their race, creed or ethnicity.

But if you were a Jew, and you saw this hit TV show with two guys in a stunt car with an SS symbol on it, named after Hitler or some other high-ranking Nazi, you might think to yourself, "Is that really necessary? Isn't this kind of like a commercial that makes the SS symbol, and thus what the Nazis were fighting for, kind of...glamorous?"

What is really prompting TV Land from pulling these reruns, like WalMart and Google no longer selling Confederate flags, is that nobody wants to be associated with it. It's bad for business, and this is a free market where consumer perception matters. So while it seems there are a lot of people online up in arms at the fact that this show is pulled, outraged that anyone should have to forsake/give up/sacrifice something they grew up with just because some people are offended, that is a mischaracterization. Imagine: choosing to act not because you have to, but because you choose not to offend others. Because maybe they have been insulted enough. That's what prompted Bubba Watson, the owner of the actual General Lee, to paint over the Confederate flag on the car with an American flag:

"@bubbawatson All men ARE created equal, I believe that so I will be painting the American flag over the roof of the General Lee #USA"

To be clear: No one is "banning" this show. There are no laws against Confederate flags in the works, though their days of flying over government property are numbered. Moreover, calling out one really old show for making Aryans look hunky is not an effort at revisionism, which seems to be a favorite allegation, or censoring or the beginning of "taking away" other old films or TV shows because of its dated mores. It's not going anywhere, and if it means so much, download all six seasons of *Dukes of Hazzard* from iTunes or get the full DVD set from Amazon. No one is banning anything, even the episodes where Tom

Wopat and John Schneider left the show over contract disputes, only to be replaced with the Dukes' "cousins," who also happened to be a brunette and blonde, but they lasted like three episodes. No one is even trying to ban guns, which is what actually killed those people in Charleston who had welcomed a stranger into Bible study.

It does not reflect upon you for liking a show that was a car ad for a big-time racist symbol. That is what inheriting culture is like. But at some point, if you are aware that something offends others, it is probably worth reflecting: why? What is so upsetting about this symbol/name/appellation? Are people wrong for being offended? These are questions even big name comics should ask themselves, as success breeds contempt for negative feedback.

Just'a good ol' boys
Never meanin' no harm.
Beats all you never saw
Been in trouble with the law
Since the day they was born
Staightnin' the curves
Flatnin' the hills
Someday the mountain might get 'em
But the law never will
Makin' their way
The only way they know how
That's just a little bit more
Than the law will allow.
Makin' their way
The only way they know how
That's just a little bit more

Than the law will allow.
Just a good ol' boy
Wouldn't change if they could
Fightin' the system like
Two modern day Robin Hood's

To review: these protagonists are criminals, but that doesn't seem necessary to stress because Jennings makes this point over and over that they are habitual offenders. What we also know for sure, as Waylon repeatedly assures us, is that these are Good Ol Boys. They would never mean harm. Though Bo and Luke Duke seem to have a propensity for blowing up stuff, particularly with a bow and arrow, but then they are like Robin Hood, and so their crimes are part of the good they do. Unrepentant and beyond reform, they wouldn't change, nor would they know how. Yet since their local law enforcement and civic authority are corrupt and inept, they don't need to comply with the government and its burdensome regulation, they can continue to run their moonshine, since they are a family of bootleggers, manufacturing and selling unlicensed intoxicants, similar to *Breaking Bad* or *True Detective*.

All this, with a Dodge Charger Confederate Flag flying through the air as its money shot, and a profile might emerge of the types of people still so invested in this overly-narrated show. Devotees of *Dukes of Hazzard* are lamenting online, "They'll never make a show like this again." Yeah, that's the point.

EPILOGUE

CHAPTER 57

Start Making Sense

Like the warning urged us, "objects in mirror may be closer than they appear." Hopefully this book offers some perspective on how the world's leading democracy became a demolition derby for an aspiring autocrat, with a future that grows cloudier by the day.

To convey what this era feels like, imagine being in an elevator that keeps going down, and every day when you hope it's going to stop, it begins dropping faster. You still have to go through each day, maintaining your routine, while your stomach fights off that falling feeling.

It still seems unfathomable to be discussing the future of American democracy with a question mark. But each day under the Trump Administration brings a jaw-dropping assertion, such as asserting that Trump could write an executive order to overturn the 14th amendment, denying birthright citizenship, something which is not remotely legal or feasible, but is a white nationalist dream come true. With stacked courts, including a stolen Supreme Court seat, who knows what checks remain to Trump's growing abuses of power?

Which brings us to the bigger problem than Trump's autocratic antics, which is that no elected Republicans will make any pretense of caring about enforcing the law. We knew from day one of Trump's term that the GOP was dropping their 'tough on crime' pretense when they allowed Trump to freely profit from his presidency, milking his secret service detail's budget with outrageous rent at Trump Tower, even gouging the agents guarding his life for the golf carts they use at his country clubs. But as Republicans have fought an investigation into Russia's role in the 2016 election, their concern over party instead of national security is more than a little disconcerting. It's hard to fault the framers for not foreseeing a constitutional crisis from so many lawmakers abetting so much lawbreaking.

While the U.S. president identifies himself as a nationalist (meaning *white* nationalist) and openly spreads conspiracy theories about Jews, many struggle to find shared recognition of how wrong this all is. The week before the 2018 midterm elections saw the greatest amount of terror in U.S. history as mail bombs were sent to over a dozen Democratic leaders, a white supremacist killed two black people at a Kroeger's grocery store in Kentucky after failing to get into a black church, and a gunman killed eleven Jews during a bris in Pittsburgh.

Exacerbating this crisis is the mainstream news, which has suffered from a false equivalency mindset and fear of being called liberal, allowing unchallenged lies to flourish over their channels. Even terrorism is blamed on both sides now: the Associated Press wrote a story about the Pittsburgh temple massacre pointing to unlocked doors as a reason it happened, despite Trump's increasingly unsubtle anti-Semitic taunts in the weeks leading up. *The New York Times* ran a story about what the targeted Democrats had said that was critical of Trump, ostensibly suggesting they had invited violence. The news that Trump wanted to overturn the 14th amendment came from an *Axios* interview where the young white male journalist grinned broadly at getting the latest scoop from the man who would be despot. It would seem impossible that we have reached this point, except that *The New York Times* has run softball profiles humanizing white supremacists and getting quotes exclusively from Trump voters in red districts about how they are supporting their president no matter what. The supposedly liberal *New York Times* repeats Trump's outrageous lies without any correction, granting them instant credibility. After the 2018 midterms, as Wisconsin Republicans hastily rewrote laws with no hearings that would severely impede the incoming Democratic governor, *The New York Times* headline was "Wisconsin Republicans Defiantly 'Stand Like Bedrock' in Face of Democratic Wins." If we ever thought the Fourth Estate would be our oversight, particularly the Paper of Record, we have the *New York Time*'s 2016 election coverage dismissing a Trump-Russia connection to remind us otherwise.

Congress and the courts are partisan refs at best, co-conspirators at worst, while journalists jockey for access to power to compete for clickbait news scoops. This leaves us with few promising options to restore the norms and values of democracy. What's more, what even counts as "democracy"? Is it a franchise, a process, a philosophical worldview?

When I first observed the Trump rallies and the growing base of his boisterous supporters, I realized something about democracy—we can marvel at the majestic principle and revere Thomas Jefferson's prose, but ultimately, democracy is really in place to keep us from killing each other.

One aspect that defines modern American Democracy is that while we hold officials to account through elections, today's body politic responds much more readily than any civilization before, through social media, cable television, late night comics, even dank memes. There are many ways to make our opinions public beyond voting, even though voting is more like a contract you offer an elected official, sealing the deal. This body politic we are in is like a fish bowl, not a vacuum.

What might prove to be a fatal aspect of American Democracy is the lack of participation in it. Half the country still doesn't vote even though they are registered, even while there are people still alive who witnessed the struggle for the vote to be granted. Voting always seemed obviously important and responsible to me growing up, so I am not someone that relates to those who refuse to participate. I get excited to vote. I'm not sure how to sell it to people more than I already have tried through movies, videos, street art, T-shirts, and stickers.

And yet that kind of pop marketing appeal might be part of the problem—campaigns become more sensationalized content which we feel free to opt out of. In America today, we are more a nation of consumers than citizens. Back when resources were scarce and infrastructure as we know it was considered luxury, people had reason to come together for their immediate future. Now more than ever, Americans exist in an insulated bubble of social media, streaming TV services, and celebrity culture.

I keep thinking of something a friend of mine told me, Ed, who was a writer on a summer reality show that had been an international hit, *I'm a Celebrity, Get Me Out Here!* The show had become a reality hit in part because of a pair of reality TV foils from MTV's *The Hills*, Spencer and Heidi, were televised throwing a fit and calling up an NBC executive to get themselves off the island because they felt their co-stars weren't sufficiently famous. The British show-runner told Ed: "We've done this show all over the world. And no one complains like Americans."

Americans complain, because we are brought up being told our voice matters, because in America we're special. "The customer is always right" is a beautiful-sounding, uniquely American assurance, emblematic of how we dream of being elevated from worker to royal providence: our social status does not matter, only our choice of where we shop. As customers we feel empowered, with major brands vying for our interest constantly, hiring our favorite athletes, licensing our favorite pop songs. The problem is, Americans think complaining is enough, and they do it a lot, but then don't actually follow through to vote and participate in the democratic process. An American is far more likely to ask for the manager than ask for their elected representative.

As such I might as well take this opportunity to briefly respond to the arguments usually offered against voting, since we still have this problem.

- **"My vote won't make a difference."** In the 2018 elections, races were decided by a single vote in Alaska, Kentucky, Illinois, and Iowa. The election of President Rutherford B. Hayes was decided by a single vote. So who knows, your vote might not be the deciding vote— but do you really need for your vote to be the deciding vote to care?

- **"I don't know enough to vote."** Well intentioned, but that doesn't negate your civic responsibility, and it sure doesn't stop people who think Jesus wrote the

Constitution from voting. It only makes their vote count more.

- **"There aren't good candidates."** No one is good enough. But there is always worse.

- **"Both parties are the same."** Sure, let's say that the Democratic Party is the lapdog of the corporatocracy— the Republican Party is the attack dog.

- **"I'm making a statement by not voting."** You are doing the opposite; no one will ever come after the non-voters to see what they want. Campaigns always go after voters that show up. Considering the increasingly brazen ways that the Republican Party is trying to restrict and prohibit voting, by not voting, you are only helping them achieve that end.

I have been struggling to put a conclusion to these essays that would be of lasting perspective at a time when it feels like we can't keep up hour-to-hour. I ultimately realized that what feels the most overwhelming—and thus the most daunting in taking action—is the idea that none of this makes sense. If we allow ourselves to buy into that, we can't figure out what to address or how to fix it.

But actually, all this does make sense.

In reality, if you follow the line of disenfranchisement going back to only 2000, there are clear turning points where the Republican Party went big on voter suppression or election fraud, holding back the country from progress despite the will of a majority of voters. This led to restrictive laws and more suppression of the vote, as the party drifted rightward, requiring increasingly drastic voter disenfranchisement as they lost the middle.

The costly mistakes that let the GOP open the doors for Trump and Putin to play house were unique hubris, as one entitled white man after another came along and thought, "I can bend the rules—just for *me*."

In 2000 & 2004, Bush and Rove banked on voter suppression in Florida and Ohio, Republican-appointed justices, and hijacking the election results before they could be reported. If I was able to cover all they did and how they did it in one film—and I am just some dude—you can bet people in other countries watched what went down and took notes. Bush and Rove thought it was fine when it was just stealing a few states for themselves.

In 2008, Senator John McCain chose a running mate without much more thought than she would be red meat to the conservative base. And boy was she—Governor Sarah Palin went from an obscure governor for half a million people to a tabloid star that would say the most insulting, patronizing things she could think of with a wink and unintentional non sequitur. McCain did not care that she was completely unqualified for civic leadership, unable to complete a full term as governor. When John McCain passed away recently, Sarah Palin was not even invited to his funeral. And yet she could have been the immediate successor to the oldest president ever, a man who just barely outlived Obama's two terms. Sarah Palin was the elevation of a wildly unqualified individual whose only political ability was blaming everything on Obama. Her predictability and over-saturation dimmed her appeal, leaving her all but forgotten by the time Obama left the White House. But looking back as to how we got a president whose only political experience was demanding a birth certificate from the first black president—John

McCain legitimizing a pageant queen demagogue is a major data point. Palin was the gateway drug to Trump.

In 2012, Mitt Romney was so smug in his unique opinion that he could say whatever he wanted, he broke new bounds in lying to the American public. He knew the base would never question him because they really just hated Obama. He took full advantage of being able to speak to crowds while not answering questions. But whereas mendacity for Mitt Romney meant lying about his or Obama's record, Trump exploited the media's reluctance to call out lies with non-stop falsehoods, so voluminous it was impossible to fact-check them all. And when the media finally did start to acknowledge Trump as a serial liar, he had already primed his base for two years by attacking journalists, saying that all unfavorable coverage was "fake news." On May 9, 2018, Trump finally acknowledged fake news is simply news he doesn't like when he tweeted: "91% of the Network News about me is negative (Fake)." Mitt Romney saw how little the base cared for him when he delivered his own unsolicited televised speech straight-up denouncing Trump during the 2016 campaign—and no one cared. Romney invoked his supposed moral authority to appeal to the very people that nominated him for president, and it blew up in his face. Those people didn't give a crap what Mitt Romney said, they wanted the guy who accused all Mexicans of being rapists.

By the time 2016 arrived, Trump had been given credibility by nonstop coverage of his demands for President Obama's birth certificate. The rest of the Republican contenders were so insincere and afraid of looking unpresidential for even a moment, they were bowled over by the guy who refused to act presidential at all. The poor, career Republicans who thought they would get by on loaded dog whistles were unprepared for an unrepentant bigot who spoke like a 1950's racist caricature. Those clueless candidates were even under the deluded notion that they had to have actual policies, like a president might. The legendary anthropologist Jane Goodall offered exquisite insight to *The Atlantic* shortly before Trump won the nomination:

"In many ways the performances of Donald Trump remind me of male chimpanzees and their dominance rituals. In order to impress rivals, males seeking to rise in the dominance hierarchy perform spectacular displays: stamping, slapping the ground, dragging branches, throwing rocks. The more vigorous and imaginative the display, the faster the individual is likely to rise in the hierarchy, and the longer he is likely to maintain that position."

That was funny during the 2016 campaign, but it stings now. Watching American citizens defer to a man who so transparently uses bluster to conceal his ineptitude, it makes you realize that many Americans really don't aspire to have a leader they believe to be superior. George W. Bush's legendary tendency to murder phrases in ways may have been embarrassing to watch, but to many in Red America, it was endearing. Those same people were suspect of Barack Obama's eloquence, insisted that Obama relied on teleprompters to be so articulate, and quick to believe in conspiracies surrounding his country of origin and his secret intentions.

Looking back at human behavior through history, we have been around long enough to recognize that no matter the technological advancements, societies are still as vulnerable to ethnic strife, authoritarian leadership, and inequality through class and gender. It's almost like just because our technology gets better, we don't become automatically more advanced in parity or diversity. I tend to think that we as Americans unconsciously equate the progress of a civil society with the progress of our devices and vehicles. Similarly, a misleading mindset in America revolves around visualizing a pendulum swing from Left to Right, side to side, as though attached to a reliable clock spanning decades.

We have seen the authoritarian streak emerge in other societies whenever it is enabled—it is not that Americans think they are different from those before, it's that we think our country was set up differently to prevent an autocrat who could consolidate power and rule like a monarch. What Trump has uncovered is that an authoritarian who actually tried could overpower the legal process we have.

Human cultures follow a cycle, one that has gone on for centuries, of banding together to meet common needs, then dividing amongst themselves in pursuit of hierarchy. The richest in society have always created exceptions for themselves. It is part of the very nature of human self-interest, as Ayn Rand would espouse, but that doesn't mean it is therefore good. It's human nature to want to kill a threat, an invader, or someone that flips you off in traffic. We all have the responsibility to control ourselves from indulging in violent or destructive behaviors.

What Trump embodies is an id that resents the very notion of self-control. Trump is the nationalist manifestation of what has always been there. The conflict before us is not Left versus Right, but belligerence vs democracy. Republicans don't want an equitable society—they are more outraged by NFL players taking a knee in brief protest than by police officers gunning down Americans without consequences. The Tea Party that was so passionate in mobilizing against deficits under Obama curiously haven't said a single thing about Trump adding $2 trillion to the federal deficit through tax cuts and government spending *on his own properties*. Republicans will insist Brett Kavanaugh's life is ruined by Dr. Christine Blasey Ford testifying to a high school assault by Kavanaugh, who went on to a lifetime appointment on the highest court of the land and a standing ovation at the Federalist Society. Dr. Ford and her family had to leave their home and go into hiding for months because of the death threats they've faced. Of course Republicans don't care about Dr. Ford, even if they believed her testimony. Republicans demand the right to have it both ways, then howl when they are told they can't.

The belligerence is the point—it's not just about a power structure that dictates different rules for how white men act, but the freedom to ignore those rules without consequence. The people at Trump rallies howling at the press pen don't care about equal or fair media coverage. They prize the opportunity to show disdain and contempt for professionals. The belligerence didn't begin with Trump —he's just more flagrant about it. The Republican Party is inherently anti-democratic because of their widespread devotion to suppressing voters. Elected leaders taking active measures to restrict their constituents' voices is as belligerent as it gets.

When I co-founded Video the Vote in 2006 and released *FREE FOR ALL!* in 2008, the subject of voter suppression was one that needed explaining, a matter no politician wanted to dive into. In 2018, Republican officials seemed to be trying to one-up each other at voter suppression, while election day coverage has turned to the numerous polling place meltdowns across the country—power outages at polling places, hundred of people waiting, voter intimidation. Trying to cast a vote today has become like the Hunger Games, with polling place struggles part of the sports coverage.

We don't discuss the psychological impact of voter suppression and stolen elections—how it makes us feel isolated, on the outskirts of our own society, how it forces us to keep fighting for things we thought we already had won. If people knew that they were on the clearly more popular side, I believe it would enhance their determination and confidence. That all of this makes sense.

The Trump cabal wants you to be confused, feel helpless, think you are alone. But the stories in these pages are here to tell you that this dark turn in America makes sense. The assault on democracy will continue, because we are still not at the point of equality where democracy isn't such a threatening concept.

What are you going to do about it?

ABOUT THE AUTHOR

John Wellington Ennis is a filmmaker and writer in Los Angeles, CA. He has been active in politics since high school in Evanston, IL. Ennis attended the film schools at USC and NYU and taught documentary filmmaking at UCLA Extension. His feature films include the Upright Citizens Brigade's *Wild Girls Gone* starring Amy Poehler and Matt Walsh, *FREE FOR ALL! One Dude's Quest to Save Our Elections*, and *PAY 2 PLAY: Democracy's High Stakes*. He co-founded the election protection group VideoTheVote.org in 2006 and served as Executive Director for Public Interest Pictures, a 501 (c)(3) dedicated to electoral reform. His first book, *Where Else But the Streets: A Street Art Dossier*, chronicles political street art in Los Angeles. He hosts "Proper Propaganda," featuring political hip hop, on Radio Free Brooklyn.

www.ingramcontent.com/pod-product-compliance
Lightning Source LLC
Chambersburg PA
CBHW040931050426
42334CB00060B/3154